STILL LOVED BY THE SUN

A RAPE SURVIVOR'S JOURNAL

MIGAEL SCHERER

SIMON & SCHUSTER

NEW YORK   LONDON   TORONTO   SYDNEY   TOKYO   SINGAPORE

SIMON & SCHUSTER
Simon & Schuster Building
Rockefeller Center
1230 Avenue of the Americas
New York, NY 10020

1 3 5 7 9 10 8 6 4 2

Library of Congress Cataloging-in-Publication Data
Still Loved by the Sun: a rape survivor's journal / Migael Scherer
p. cm.
1. Scherer, Migael   2. Rape victims—United States.   I. Title.
HV6561.S34A3   1992
362.88'3'092—dc20
[B]   91-15138
CIP
ISBN 0-671-76785-2

*The author gratefully acknowledges permission from the following sources to reprint
material in their control:*
Doubleday for lines from "Waking," from *The Collected Poems of Theodore
Roethke,* copyright © 1948 by Theodore Roethke.
HarperCollins Publishers for lines from "Elm," from *The Collected Poems of
Sylvia Plath,* copyright © 1963 by The Estate of Sylvia Plath.
W. W. Norton & Company for lines from "Apologia pro Poemate Meo,"
from *Wilfred Owen, The Complete Poems and Fragments,* edited by Jon Stallwor-
thy, copyright © 1963 and 1983 by The Executors of Harold Owen's Estate.
Oxford University Press for lines from "The Room," from *Collected Poems by
Conrad Aiken,* copyright © 1953, 1971 by Conrad Aiken; renewed 1981 by
Mary Aiken.
Peters Fraser & Dunlop for lines from "Lessons of the War," from *A Map of
Verona* by Henry Reed.
Random House for lines from "Musee des Beaux Arts," from *W. H. Auden,
Collected Poems,* edited by Edward Mendelson, copyright © 1940, renewed
1968, by W. H. Auden.

For Kimberly,
who never had the chance to speak.
And for my husband,
whose love helped me to do so.

AUTHOR'S NOTE

The people in this book are real. In order to protect them and their privacy, all names, except my own, have been changed. Some place names have also been changed, most notably the name of the laundromat.

I thank everyone who helped me through the events described here and encouraged me as I wrote, including the friends and family members who are not portrayed. I am also grateful to the women in my support group who generously allowed me to tell their stories. All but "Lisa's" are true; hers is a composite of those in the group I was unable to contact, and of others who offered details of their own assaults.

Writing this book required that I examine painful events I was often unaware I was avoiding. My guides through this process deserve special thanks: Phyllis Hatfield, for her meticulous editing and enthusiasm; Beth Vesel, for her candid first response and continued interest; Dan Levant, for his honesty and persistence; Gail Winston at Simon & Schuster, for coaching me through the final steps. And most especially my agent Elizabeth Wales, for her extraordinary efforts that made it all happen.

CONTENTS

|

REMOVED

Violence shall synchronize your movements like a tune . . .

—W. H. AUDEN

St. Martin, Virgin Islands
February 17, 1988

Dear Anna,

Paul will send you a postcard of St. Martin that shows
the Caribbean blue you described when I visited you in
Portland two weeks ago. You probably won't get it
until after you receive this letter, which I will mail from
the States on our way back to Seattle. It bears news I
want you, my friend, to learn as soon as possible.

Last Tuesday morning, while loading three dryers in
my Ballard neighborhood laundromat, I was grabbed
from behind, dragged with a knife at my throat into the
machine room behind the dryers, raped, and strangled
close to death. Lord knows how or why I survived with
so little damage: cuts and a carved heart on my neck,

1

deeper cuts on my hands, bruises, my sanity intact (apparently). *He* simply said I was "a very lucky woman" as his hands unclenched. The guy, by the way, was your average blondish thirty-five-year-old from whom I sensed no danger when I first entered the Kwik-Kleen or when I returned from grocery shopping at Safeway just before the wash cycle was done.

So. The rest of the morning and into the afternoon I spent at the police station, giving a complete description of the attack to the officer who had responded to my 911 call. The experience of reliving it minute by minute proved remarkably therapeutic, actually. Once home at our boat (the cop carried in my groceries and laundry) I called Paul (not in his office), Margaret (in a meeting), and Jack. It took Jack less than five minutes to arrive; he never let go of me until he and I picked up Margaret and the three of us walked into Paul's office. By this time I was numb but still functioning. Next step was to Group Health for the postassault exam, a dizzying combination of gentle medical attention and rigorous evidence gathering. Approximately two hours of it.

The next two days I was never alone, nor was I ever far from feelings of terror and shock. Getting ready for this Caribbean vacation was unreal. It took me all day Thursday to pack and pay some bills between bouts of uncontrollable shivering, nausea, and sobbing. Paul's sister Chris was with me, urging me to eat, keeping me warm, holding me. When I walked off *Orca* to go to the airport I forgot my bag. Around me everyone picked up the pieces, the details of living that I was incapable of remembering.

My first normal responses occurred with jet lag. Here at last was a disorientation I could understand. All went smoothly until Puerto Rico, where a flight was canceled and we were bumped off another. In the airport over a Bloody Mary I was finally ready to tell Paul every-thing that had occurred in those twenty minutes Tuesday morning. He covered his face with his hands and cried.

By the time our friends John and Barbara met us in St. Martin I was exhausted, jumpy, thrilled. Since then I have been in the embrace of heaven. The house they are building is an airy, marble-floored villa overlooking the mountains and saltwater lagoon on the west side of St. Martin. A white-and-azure beach is five minutes' walk away. We have sunned and snorkeled and talked and read and sailed. We are eating late dinners, energetically discussing politics, economics, cruising, and traveling (almost everyone who lives here comes from someplace else). Of course, we told them what had happened so they could understand my otherwise baffling moments of anxiety and introspection. They are not intimate friends. Their healthy instincts are to keep smiles on our faces, to steer the conversation away from painful memories, and to be protective.

Every day I feel calmer and stronger. I am reminded of nineteenth-century novels in which the heroine recovers from a long illness at a seaside spa, languorously breathing warm salt air and gazing at the horizon. Inside, just as languorously, swims a shark whose unpredictable surfacings terrify me. I'm not sure the shark will ever leave, so I am content to learn to move aside as it rushes past.

I think about my size a lot these days. Believe it or not, I have always considered myself to be a big person. Even, perhaps, a bit formidable. Didn't I, shoulder to shoulder with Paul, build the boat that is now our home? Didn't I—for years—control a classroom full of high-school kids? I scarcely believe it, for now I feel vulnerable and small. I continually ask Paul if I am that woman's size or that girl's size. And you know what? Most women are bigger than me! What a target I must have been, hauling in my basket of laundry with such bravado.

3

Paul has been marvelous. We are loving each other a lot these days. To an outsider we must look like newlyweds. Every day and every experience has a beautiful crispness to me, every new friendly face is a treasure, every trusted friend a safe haven. I took so much for granted before.

This is the first letter I have written since that morning. It has been hard, but it has helped a lot. And it could only be written to you.

Love,
Migael

SUNDAY, FEBRUARY 21

Not quite two weeks have passed since my world was ripped apart by a sharp knife at my neck, a low voice in my ear, and wild hands on my body and around my throat. Now I sit surrounded by Caribbean softness: cotton upholstery beneath my bare legs, trade winds through the open walls of this room, green mountains on the far side of the lagoon. I am at peace for the moment. Within the half hour Paul and I will take off for dinner and an evening exploring. I am astonished to find myself looking ahead to the next activity with anything but confusion.

Today has been the closest to normal I have felt since I started loading those three dryers. The shark swimming within me has been very quiet today (resting for his next ambush, no doubt). I felt stirrings of curiosity this afternoon and walked the perimeter of the house by myself!

TUESDAY, FEBRUARY 23

The final leg of the journey home to Seattle. Our flights have all been on time. Customs and immigration went smoothly in Puerto Rico. During our three-hour layover in Atlanta Paul and I sat in comfortable chairs, sipping beer.

Leaving St. Martin was hard. Anxiety hit late last night, just before the wind picked up. From habit, I suppose, I began to think about what I'd be doing during the coming week. The thought paralyzed me. I am suddenly unable to plan more than one day at a time. I am also afraid of returning to Seattle, a city that has always been home to me but now triggers memories of violence and pain. I had learned to feel safe in St. Martin, was just beginning to feel independent, and now must start over. It will be difficult, I think, but at least I've had some practice, however contrived.

I keep imagining that I will step off this plane in Seattle and into the custody (protective? investigative?) of a police officer. Then I would be pulled into the depths, deep enough to see the shark clearly, and recall the frenzy of his attack. My hope is that my attacker, my almost-killer, has been swallowed up himself and will not strike again anywhere, ever. Reality is no doubt somewhere between these two projections. Just please let me have sufficient time to heal and strengthen. I will need more courage than I have now to take this next step.

But what a reprieve I have had! Ten full days of warmth and friendliness. How indulged I have been; it is no wonder I am already beginning to function somewhat normally, only two weeks to the day afterward.

THURSDAY, FEBRUARY 25

All day yesterday I dreaded the night. Paul had offered to go alone, but I needed to be there too, to break the news to my parents. It wasn't my mother who worried me. I knew she would be shocked, then loving, like Paul's mom. It was my father. All I could think of, suddenly, was him at the head of the dinner table when I was a child, telling me to sit up straight and chew with my mouth closed. And when I cried, to go to my room. Where would my attack fit into his ordered life?

"Just tell them what happened," Paul said during the long drive to their house. "You don't have to go into detail. They won't want that anyway. I'll be right next to you. And we won't stay long." He held my hand as he drove, squeezing his confidence into me.

My parents answered the door together, invited us in, offered to take our coats. "You're so tan," my mother said, giving me a quick hug. "Did you have a good time in St. Martin?"

"Come on in," my father said, directing us into the living room, past the carefully arranged books on the dusted shelves. He sat back into his chair and picked up a magazine from the neat stack on the small table to his right. He opened it on his lap.

Paul and I sat on the raised granite hearth, our backs to the empty fireplace, our bodies touching. My mother sat on the couch opposite us. She leaned forward, waiting. I couldn't bear to look at her.

"We have some bad news," Paul began. "Two days before we left for our vacation, Migael was attacked." My mother sat motionless. My father continued to page through his magazine. "You might want to put that down," Paul said to him. "This is important. Migael was raped. She was strangled. She was cut up."

I leaned against Paul and looked at my parents. My mother looked from me to Paul and back to me. My father looked only at Paul.

"Where did it happen?" he asked.

This time I spoke. "I was in a laundromat, in Ballard. In the morning."

"Are you all right now?" he asked.

"Yes," I said, eager to reassure him. "I went to the hospital afterward. None of the cuts required stitches. They're all healed up now. I reported it to the police," I added, anticipating his next question.

My mother made a soft sound, like a whimper. She rose from the couch and reached for me. Holding my face in her hands, she kissed me on both cheeks. "Oh," she said. "Oh, Migael."

"Isn't the coffee about ready?"

At the sound of my father's voice my mother straightened, clasped her hands together, and moved toward the kitchen. I could hear her opening cupboards and drawers, setting cups and spoons on a tray.

"Your mother made dessert," my father said as she served us. "Would you like some?" Paul and I shook our heads. My mother returned to her seat on the couch. Like me, she did not pick up her cup.

"You know," my father observed, "this happened to your cousin Lynn."

"Yes," I said dully. "I remember hearing about it. It must have been horrible for her."

"Did you ever talk about it with Lynn's mom?" Paul asked.

My father shook his head quickly, as if such a conversation with his sister was out of the question. "She didn't say much," he answered. "But we both decided not to tell Mother. Your grandmother was pretty old then," he explained to me. "It would have upset her."

"Well," Paul said, "we thought it was important that you hear about Migael's attack from us, directly. We didn't have a chance before we left. To tell the truth, we were in shock then." He quickly finished his coffee. "We need to get home. We're both real tired."

"Yes," my father said, standing up abruptly. "That jet lag sticks with you, doesn't it?" He moved with us to the door. My mother brought us our coats.

"Take care of yourself," she said, zipping up my jacket, brushing back my hair. "I'll pray for you every day. You too, Paul," she said, turning to him. "This is hard on you too."

"Thanks," Paul said as he put his arms around her. "Don't be afraid to call me."

"We're really sorry it happened," my father said at the door. "Let us know if there's anything we can do, won't you?" He shook Paul's hand. He gave me a stiff, brief hug.

"You did real well," Paul said when we were back in the car.

"Real well. Even when he kept looking at that damn magazine."

I stared out at the wet streets. The rain, and a sudden, intense sorrow, blurred the lights. "That was the first time," I said slowly.

"First time? What do you mean, first time?"

I was crying now. "That was the first time my father ever hugged me."

2

"LUCKY WOMAN"

And the various holds and rolls and throws and breakfalls
Do not depend on any sort of weapon,
But only on what I might coin a phrase and call
The ever-important question of human balance
And the ever-important need to be in a strong
Position at the start.

—HENRY REED
"Lessons of the War"

TUESDAY, MARCH 1

Tuesday again, my first back in Seattle since *that* Tuesday. Same kind of day—gray, drizzly—and at about 8:30 I began to get jumpy. At 9:30, exactly the time I'd headed for the Kwik-Kleen three weeks ago, I walked to the mailbox and then, without thinking, into Jack's office at the shipyard.

Jack was sitting, slightly hunched, over a desk cluttered

with tools and catalogs. His black mustache and beard worked back and forth across his face as he searched for the part he needed. He was wearing the navy blue nylon vest and the threadbare chamois shirt he had worn that Tuesday. The feelings I had then—relief, safety, and a powerful attachment—flooded over me. Jack turned and smiled.

"Well hello," he said, and immediately he stood up and enveloped me in a welcoming hug. The cranes on the loading dock screeched. Phones rang. The marine radio on his windowsill squawked. I sighed with relief as I walked back to *Orca* at 10:30.

Now I sit just up the hill from our marina, at Stan and Teri's, my laundry washing and drying in their basement. "You'll be needing these now," Teri had said, handing me the keys to their house, knowing I will not be using the laundromat—any laundromat—for some time. Knowing also that I would take up the challenge the inevitable pile of dirty clothes would present despite Paul's offer to do the laundry "forever" (or his sister's wry suggestion: "Let 'em rot," Chris said). What friends! Paul and I had turned to them instinctively the day after the attack. I had spent that afternoon with Stan, never more than a few feet from him. The fact that he and Teri are therapists helps, I know, but equally reassuring are the details of their lives: the dog sleeping in the dining room, the magnetized letters scattered at knee height on their refrigerator, the boys' rocking horse in front of the living room window. Sheltered in their home, I am wary as I measure the soap and bend over their washing machine, but I am content. I seem to have recaptured a bit of the satisfaction that completing a simple chore (or what used to be a simple chore) gives me.

I have such mixed feelings about February, which is over at last. It was always such a short, easy month to get through, even those four winters in Alaska, even last year when Paul took the architect job here, transferring from his position in Juneau, and I stayed behind to get the boat ready to cruise to Seattle in the summer. This year February began with a solo drive to Portland to visit Anna, just four months into her widowhood. It ended with her kindness to me when I received her flowers and poignant message: "Thank goodness for your life."

What I am missing most these days is a sense of control. Yesterday morning's phone calls and sortings were such pathetic attempts at my former efficiency. I am unable to initiate anything. In St. Martin this quality fit right in, but in Seattle, surrounded by things-to-do, I find it—well, only mildly annoying actually. See how passive I have become?

At least I can be alone for longer periods of time now: yesterday until 2:00 P.M. (including my first walk alone to the mailbox, only two blocks away) and for what looks like most of today, with intermittent breaks. I feel steady, growing strength.

Events like last night's erode the strength. Gary and Sandra came over, with flowers, beer, wine, and good wishes. And into the boat with them came the unstated fact that our friendship has changed. The party-time aura they exuded, which has been the basis of our ten-year friendship, grated on me.

They asked a few questions about my attack, but didn't want to hear the details. Exuberant as always, Sandra went on and on about how dangerous the world is and all the precautions she takes to be safe. I crawled into a corner and tried to appear interested as she enthusiastically described assaults she had heard about from other women. By nine o'clock I wanted them to leave, to stop chatting and drinking as though there were something to celebrate. I had no energy to be social. Their conversation left me behind, exhausted and sad.

What a contrast to my feelings around friends like Margaret and Jack, who strengthen rather than sap me. Jack's face, which I first saw over twenty years ago in the high school he and Paul and I attended, comforts me immediately. He holds me with his eyes. He doesn't wait for me to ask for his words or touch. Nor does Margaret. She calls *me*, patiently listens to my evasive reassurances that I'm doing fine, gently asks the questions that allow me to uncover my feelings rather than hide them. Of course it drains me to talk about the attack, but it calms me as well. And it is always better with someone whose instincts are simple, warm, and direct, than with those who generalize or, without knowing, try to minimize my pain.

I think the shark is undergoing some kind of change. Perhaps I have been too busy and distracted by others to feel his motion. His frenzied surfacings are less frequent. It is the aftermath of his attack that has gained prominence now: confusion, sleeplessness, and agitation.

WEDNESDAY, MARCH 2

Yesterday I called Detective Peters to inquire about the case and heard the news: He is still at large and has struck again. Same description, same insistence on masturbation. This time, a woman alone at home and he in a white ski mask. Same knife, no doubt. No strangling attempt, thank god. So now the hunt steps up, in tidy Scandinavian Ballard.

And it all rushed back. There was that hard face, those flat, almost dusty eyes, inches from mine. And the breath of a cigarette smoker in my nostrils, and the sunlight through the open, barred windows. I trembled a moment, sitting at the chart table, then broke down, sobbing.

A few minutes later I was talking with Margaret. I don't even remember dialing her number. I calmed in the wash of her matter-of-fact, gentle voice.

Then did I attack my morning job with a vengeance: cleaning the boat's head. I scrubbed, bleached, and polished. It was even more therapeutic than pulling apart pallet boards last night for the aft-cabin remodeling project, though not as pleasurably violent. I thought of Paul's maxim: "When the going gets tough, the tough clean bathrooms." I felt stronger again.

But in bed last night the face came back. I squeezed my eyes shut, trying to blot it out. I lay on my side and curled into a tight ball. Go away, I begged. *Please.*

"You're back there again, aren't you, honey?" Paul turned and wrapped himself around me. I relaxed slightly at the feel of his warm stomach against my back and the weight of his left arm across my chest, pressing me to him. "Is it better when I hold you like this?"

"Yes," I said. "But inside my head, it's like a movie. Worse than a movie. And I can't turn it off."

Paul snuggled even closer. "You need someone to change the reel for you," he said.

"Oh yeah?" A sudden image of Paul in high school, running the projector at the back of the darkened classroom, made me smile. "Which reel do you have in mind?"

"The ocean," he whispered. "Off Baranof Island."

We raised anchor early, not knowing how far we'd get that day and not really concerned about it. We had the ocean on our minds. It had been more than a week since we'd been out there, when a northerly had carried us south down the outside of Chichagof Island into Salisbury Sound. Sails up almost all the way into Sitka, all of them, the genoa and the main and the mizzen, wing-in-wing-in-wing. *Orca* had flown in a hiss of sea foam.

On this morning we motored out through the rocks that crowd the northern shore of Baranof Island, counting off buoys, eyes moving from the charts to the shore to the depth sounder. As before, the ocean was waiting for us. *Orca* rose to meet the swells. The northerly had weakened. A dark band on the horizon, and the confused seas, promised a squall or two. I pulled my wool cap over my ears. I pulled on my fingerless gloves. "Another beautiful July day sailing in Alaska," Paul said. We both laughed.

"Let's put up the yankee," I said, needlessly as it turned out, since Paul was already heading for the starboard foredeck where the smaller headsail was stowed. I pointed *Orca* into the wind and switched on the autopilot. As Paul released the sail stops I wrapped the halyard around the winch and raised the sail. My arms strained with the effort. By the time we reached Seattle they would be brown and strong.

"And a reefed main," Paul yelled from the mainmast. The raised yankee, flogging in the wind, snapped loudly. Without a word we raised the mainsail, Paul's movements and mine perfectly synchronized. Without a word I turned the wheel as Paul eased out the sheets. *Orca* faltered a moment, as though looking for the wind. With a soft shudder her sails filled and she headed south.

All morning we watched that dark band on the horizon, wishing it farther to the west. The clouds above it were full of rain, and the wind there 30 knots—more than we wanted to handle. We watched the sky, listened to the weather report, checked the barometer. We tracked our position on the chart. We could run for shelter if we needed, but only if we knew exactly where we were. The rocky, convoluted shore of Baranof Island was as ready to crush as to embrace us.

By noon the northerly had steadied. The dark line thinned and, finally, disappeared. White cumulus clouds retreated to the west. Through the binoculars we saw the horizon, crowded with trawlers, explode into diamonds as the sun penetrated the haze. A flock of murrelets skimmed the water, their wings beating rapidly. A startled puffin surfaced and dove. An otter, cradled on its back, all but waved. To the east Baranof Island rose, deeply green, from the sea. Beneath us *Orca* rocked gently homeward.

FRIDAY, MARCH 4

My brother's visit yesterday afternoon left me feeling empty, almost transparent. Charles sat on the ladder of the companionway and calmly explained about the pressures in his own life and how the news of my attack affected him. "I haven't told her yet," he said, speaking of his wife. "It's going to be really hard. She's had some rough times lately. And the kids are a handful." Instead of easing the pain, Charles's words seemed to increase it. The description of his own troubles was no comfort, but rather a heavy, extra burden. I stared dully as he spoke, and was relieved when he left. I curled up on the windowseat in the pilothouse and cried.

I woke this morning confused, hurt, and exhausted. In an attempt to help myself, I called the mental-health clinic at Group Health. The pamphlet I had been given in the emergency room said they had specially trained therapists. Hoping that the certainty of an appointment would steady me, I dialed the number. The woman who answered took my name. "What is this concerning?" she asked. I tried to keep my voice even as I explained, but my spirits plunged when I was transferred and then put on hold. Alarmed at the sudden panic that rose to the surface, I hung up. Someone called me back, patiently talked me through my tears, and arranged an appointment early next week. I am weak, weaker than I thought. And I am afraid.

Anna's visit later in the day shored me up. She had made the long drive from Portland to, as she explained, look at me, touch me, talk with me face to face. She sat across from me at the galley table; the flowers she had sent earlier in the week filled the space between us. I moved them aside. At this table we had sipped many glasses of wine, discussed books and teaching, shared travel stories. Her marriage and move to Portland, and our move to Juneau, had only enriched the friendship. Sorrow deepened it further. Six months ago I sat in her home, on the bed where her husband lay dying of cancer, full of love for them both. Now she sat with me.

Unafraid, Anna asked for the details. "What happened at the police station?" she wanted to know. "And what about the hospital? Was it as bad as they say?"

I hesitated a moment. I desperately wanted to tell her everything.

"I was very lucky," I began.

"Are you badly hurt?" he asked, standing at the open door of the patrol car he had emerged from so suddenly. "I can take you to a hospital right now." All of his dark-blue energy seemed to focus on me alone. Behind him blue lights flashed. I heard urgent voices from a radio, and a siren. The laundromat across the street, the boat shop, and the telephone behind me seemed to disappear.

"I'm OK," I said. "I'm OK." My eyes fixed on his face for one long moment as my fingers, sticky and bloody, struggled with the unbuttoned fly of my jeans. Had I always been so small? He opened the back door of his car and I stepped in.

I sat stiffly on the edge of the seat, my knees drawn up, my body folded forward over my thighs. "I'm having my period," I said into my hands. "Maybe that's why he didn't kill me . . ."

All I could see of the police officer in front of me was the back of his head, his black hair, occasionally his right profile. Mostly I stared at the back of his seat as the car zigzagged inexplicably through side streets. His questions were simple, rapid, probably routine: What color are his eyes? His hair? How tall is he? How much does he weigh? What was he wearing? Did I notice a car? He moved his head from side to side, as though searching for the man I described. Beneath the questions I heard anger and impatience, but it was not directed at me. "I just drove by!" he said. "I just drove by and never looked!"

He turned a corner and we were back where it had begun. "You're doing really well," he said. "I'd like to get a complete description from you of what happened. Will you do that for me at the station?"

"Yes," I answered, remembering the lesson I had repeated so often to my high-school journalism students: Write it down immediately; within twelve hours the details will have faded. My face was wet with tears. My left hand pressed the scratchy paper towel against the wounds on my neck.

He stopped the car in front of the boat shop I had called from; someone came out and handed me the burgundy jacket I had left on the floor. I put it on, reassured by its warmth, aware for the first time that I was cold. "I want to go in there," the cop explained as he parked across the street, in front of the laundromat. "Sometimes these guys leave their wallets." I followed closely, eyes on the gun at his hip. I saw an overturned chair, a streak of blood on the floor. My blood, I noted, not feeling anything. The police uniform seemed to fill the narrow room behind the dryers as I numbly followed him. He stopped, turned abruptly, guided me back out into the laundromat. But I had seen what his body had only partly obscured: a blood-tipped tampon on the floor, an overturned stack of metal chairs, white with red spots.

"He took my underpants," I said, as though that was his most incomprehensible act. I hesitated in front of the three dryers I had been loading, bewildered.

"Look," the cop said. "Let's get these clothes going. I can drive you to the station, get your statement, and they'll be dry when I bring you back. How do you like these sorted?" He quickly tossed the rest of my wet laundry into the dryers, his dark eyes on my face.

"You've done this before, haven't you?" I said, groping for the roll of quarters in my jacket pocket, relieved at the feel of my car keys and the crumpled bills.

"Sure," he said, taking the roll from my hand. "I've been married a long time. How many quarters do you use?" His fingers clawed at the orange paper wrapping. The skin of his hands was olive, the hair dark at his wrists. He wore a black watch.

"Three in those two," I answered, pointing, "and two in there." He inserted the coins, flipped the knobs. The dryer motors roared softly, tumbling the damp clothing. As we left I saw the folded newspaper the sandy-haired man had been reading so calmly.

The precinct station was spacious, airy, unbelievably peaceful. My eyes passed over the blue uniforms of officers absorbed in their quiet routines. I felt invisible. The cop at my side seemed taller, jumpier, more aware of himself. "Do you want to use a bathroom to wash your hands?" he asked, walking me past gray counters and desk cubicles, down a short hall. He knocked on a door, announced my presence, nodded at me to go on in. "I've got some calls to make," he said. "I'll be waiting for you."

I stepped in cautiously. At the row of sinks I rinsed my hands; the bleeding had slowed. I closed my stiff left hand over a clean paper towel. I avoided my reflection in the mirror. Ducking into a stall, I mechanically pulled down my jeans, sat on the toilet. A sour smell rose from the body I no longer felt was my own.

I sat beside him at a round table, in a quiet, open room flooded with daylight. He had taken off his dark-blue jacket, had placed his hand-held radio and a stack of paper in front of him. With quiet patience he asked his questions, filling each blank on the form with firm strokes of his ballpoint pen. RAPE, he printed in bold capital letters and, then, ARMED ROBBERY.

What I had been willing to describe I now found unbelievably difficult to face. Each question opened a door I wanted to lock forever, each gentle prompting put into focus what so much of me wanted to make cloudy. "This must be very hard for you to do," I said, almost whispering. "I don't want to remember."

"You're doing a great job," he said, his face open, his eyes soft. "What happened next?" I continued on.

When it was done he stacked the pages in order and sighed: "That was a long one." Ignoring my refusal, he brought me a soft drink, popped the pull-tab, watched me drink. "Now, what about injuries?" he asked. "Did you check when you were in the bathroom?"

I nodded, resisting this new direction. My body seemed so far away. I didn't want to think about it. "I'm OK," I said.

"It's important that you see a doctor today." His voice was calm but insistent. "I'll call ahead for you if you like. No? Is

there someone who can go with you? Please don't go alone."
He paused. "May I see your hand?"

I placed my clenched left hand into the open palm he offered, slowly unfolded it, removed the crumpled paper towel.
Every crease of skin was etched a dull red. My fingers
throbbed, crisscrossed with red cuts. One gaped widely.

Releasing my hand, he gingerly lifted my hair from my
neck. His fingers brushed my wet cheek as he tucked my hair
behind my ear.

"Oh," he said, in a voice that no longer sounded matter-of-
fact. "It's a heart. You've been carved."

All the names in my address book blurred together as I
stood at the chart table aboard *Orca*. Who were all these people? Who among them could I call, who among them would
believe me instantly, who was home in the middle of the
afternoon? I stared stupidly at the ship's clock, unable to read
the time. I thought of forgetting the whole thing, of carrying
on with the day as though nothing had happened. The groceries I had bought earlier in the morning and the clean, crumpled laundry were strewn about the main cabin; there was
plenty for me to do. But I couldn't shake the steady gaze of the
police officer who had helped me carry those bundles down
the dock. Or his parting words: "Get to the hospital today.
Promise? And don't go by yourself." I had nodded as I shook
his hand. I had promised.

But Paul had left his office, and Margaret was at a meeting,
and only the machine answered at Stan and Teri's. Its recorded
message nearly shattered my fragile resolve. I knew who to call
next, but hesitated. I pictured the pace of his small office, filled
with questions from yard crew about hoses, motors, and lu-
bricating oils, and the more urgent problems from the crews of
boats at sea. I took a deep breath and dialed Jack's number.

"Yeah," he answered, ready for the next problem.

"This is Migael." I paused, then plunged ahead. "I just got

back from the police station. I was raped this morning, and strangled, and I can't get hold of Paul." There. I had said it.

"Where are you?" he asked, his voice flat, anxious.

"Home," I replied. "On the boat." The telephone was suddenly heavy in my hand.

"I'll be there in a minute," he said.

I dropped the receiver into its cradle, then mechanically walked down to the galley and stowed the groceries. Soothed by the routine, I smoothed and folded each brown sack. Outside I laid the dock cart sideways on the cabin trunk. Looking up as I did so, I saw Jack approach from the parking lot.

All in one smooth motion he put his cigarette in his mouth and swung around the barbed wire of the locked marina gate. When had he become so big? I walked toward him on the dock, my hands hanging at my sides, as his were. He threw his cigarette in the water and reached for me.

"Oh," he said. "Your neck . . ."

"It was so awful," I moaned, encircled now by his arms. I buried my face against him. I collapsed into his embrace.

The low yellow lights just inside the emergency entrance helped, but I still didn't want to go in, would have preferred the cold rain of that early dark evening. With Paul's arm tight around my shoulders, and Jack and Margaret's silent presence behind me, I was quietly moved toward the double doors. They all fell away as the white-haired nurse guided me through the bright hall into the examining room.

Numbly, I sat down on the swivel chair, a cabinet on my left, the examining table on my right and, beyond, a long counter. I shivered intermittently and felt the slow tears I had been absently smearing across my cheeks for so long.

The nurse walked to the counter and brought back a large tray crowded with instruments and bottles and cups. "This has happened before, hasn't it?" I said.

"I'm afraid so," she answered, her lips upturned in a brief smile. She spoke with a soft Austrian accent. Her movements

were deliberate, but slow and gentle. Her uniform was won-
derfully white. "When did this happen?" she asked as she
wrapped the cuff around my arm and took my blood pressure.

"This morning," I said. "In a laundromat. In Ballard."

"Ballard?" She shook her head in disbelief, stripped off the
cuff. "Are you going to report it?"

"I already have," I said, puzzled at the question. Reaching
into my jacket pocket, I retrieved one of the cards the officer
had given me, looking at it for the first time. Seattle Police
Department, it read beside a blue and black symbol. In heavy
block letters the cop had printed his name, MIKE CRISTO,
and a string of numbers. I was startled at the date scrawled
across the bottom, 2-9-88, and at the time, 1030 HRS. What
time was it now? I handed the card to the nurse. She studied it
briefly, made a few notes on her clipboard, and passed it back
to me.

"This morning," she said, almost to herself. A pause, then,
slowly: "The main purpose of this exam is to check your
injuries, to test you for disease, to take care of *you*. But the
doctor and I will also collect evidence. When you're on the
table we'll turn out the lights and shine this"—she pulled a
black searchlight from the cabinet—"between your legs. It'll
illuminate any sperm in that area. We'll take some fluids from
your vagina, and do a wash after."

"He didn't rape me with his penis," I said, as though apologizing for all the effort she described. "He used his hand." His
hands. I could feel the rough course they had made over my
body, and the awakening of soreness everywhere, and pain.
"He strangled me," I explained, reaching for my neck. "It
hurts."

"Let's get your coat off," the nurse said. Her hands on my
shoulders were like a caress. "We'll need to do everything in
any case. If we miss one item, and he's caught, he might get
off." Her voice hardened at these last words, but the softness
returned as she continued. She handed me a plastic cup with a
lid. "Take this to the bathroom across the hall. We need a urine
sample to determine if you are pregnant now." I nodded,

followed her directions. She was behind me as I entered the bathroom, and waiting for me when I emerged.

"Now," she said when we were back in the examining room, "we'll need all your clothes off. Here's a robe. It ties in the back." She left the room.

The robe was warm when it touched my skin, a blue-and-white cotton that was immediately comforting. My fingers fumbled uselessly with the ties. Scooting on to the examining table, I noted gratefully that it was covered with cloth, not paper. The room was bright but not glaring.

The nurse walked in, laden with white blankets. "Here," she said, wrapping them around my shoulders and covering my bare legs. The blankets were warm, as though they had just been pulled from a hot dryer.

"Oh," I sighed, all of me relaxing into their embrace. Moments later I was shivering uncontrollably.

The door opened and Paul entered, a blur of black and gray with dark-blue eyes, unbelievably real. Standing in front of me, he stroked my arm and gently held the hands that lay heavy on my lap. "Jack and Margaret are out there with me," he explained. "I've been making some calls. How are you doing?"

"I'm cold," I said, and he tucked the blankets more firmly around me.

"We're waiting," he said as he left. "We're all thinking of you."

The nurse had begun to roll my clothes into brown paper sacks, one item per sack. "The police will pick these up for evidence," she explained. "There may be some clues here. Were you wearing the jacket?" She set it aside on a hook when I shook my head. I wondered what I would wear when I left, but could not hold the thought. She carried the sacks to the counter, where she began to label them.

The door opened again and a tall, fair man in a white coat entered, a clipboard in one hand. "I'm the doctor," he said simply. "Can you tell me what happened?"

"He raped me," I said. Still sitting on the edge of the examining table, I looked up into his face but did not see it. My mind was filled with the other face that had looked down at me with so much hate. "He had a knife. He strangled me. It hurts to breathe," I added, noticing for the first time a painful hoarseness.

The doctor nodded and took my left hand, opened it, studied the raw red cuts. So slowly he seemed not to move at all, he lifted my chin, brushed back my hair, touched my neck with his fingertips. My eyes searched his face, but it revealed nothing. His hand moved lightly over the bruises on my left shoulder. He moved to the counter and wrote on his clipboard. I sagged and closed my eyes.

"OK," he said, turning back to me. "Can you lie down now?" The nurse moved to help me, to rearrange the blankets over me. She placed each of my feet in the stirrups, which were covered with lambskin. Soft.

I barely felt the instruments or the gloved hand. I didn't want to remember that other hand. I didn't want to remember the terror. I closed my eyes and listened to my shallow breathing, the clink of metal and glass, the rustle of cloth. The room went dark; I could feel the heat of the spotlight on my thighs.

"Everything's fine," the doctor said when the lights went on. I sighed, unaware until that moment that I had been so anxious. He lowered my feet from the stirrups and helped me sit up. Slumped on the edge of the table, I watched the two of them at the counter, their white backs to me, as they murmured to one another and wrote on their charts. They seemed to be giving each other directions, checking from a long list.

The doctor turned. "I'll give you something for those cuts," he said. His face was tired, resigned. He left.

A loud knock on the door. The nurse rushed past me, opened it slightly. I glimpsed the blue uniforms of two police officers, heard the squeak of equipment on their hips, sensed their restless energy. The nurse closed the door, hurried to finish labeling the sacks of my clothing.

Paul appeared, a Styrofoam cup in his hand, smiling uncertainly. "Here," he said, "it's frozen yogurt. Eat some." He lifted a spoonful to my mouth, then handed me the cup. I ate it all.

The nurse approached us holding a round specimen dish and a small sharpened wooden stick. "Fingernails," she explained. "I'd like to clean under your fingernails." She took my left hand and scraped the blackness beneath the nails, delicately tapping the scrapings into the dish. Was it all blood? Was any of it his?

"Could you lie back down?" the nurse asked. She stood over me with a small black comb, uncovered me, and slowly combed my pubic hair. I felt the fine teeth pull gently against my skin and thought: All of this would have been done to me if I were dead.

The nurse returned to the counter as I sat back up, wrote a few more notes, retrieved a Polaroid camera. Paul held my hair back as she snapped photos of my neck, none of which came out in focus. She seemed relieved when I told her the ones taken at the precinct had been very clear.

"We're almost done," she announced, walking toward the door with the paper sacks. "I'll be right back." Paul remained at my side. His eyes never left my face.

A man entered with a tray that clinked with tubes and syringes. He drew blood from my left arm, his eyes full of questions. I did not feel the tourniquet or the needle, or hear the explanation he gave.

The nurse returned with a tube of ointment which she squeezed onto her fingertips and deftly applied to my neck and left hand. "Let's get you dressed," she said, standing me up, fastening the back ties of the hospital gown. "You can take this with you." She wrapped a short striped robe around me, tied it in front. I pulled on the dark-blue sweater Paul had brought, pulled up my knee socks, put my arms in the jacket that had somehow become so large. My knees and lower thighs protruded, naked. I flinched at the thought of the cold night outside.

The nurse left and another woman entered. "I'm the social worker," she said. "I understand you've been through a horrible experience." She tried to draw me out, but I couldn't follow her words. Tears spilled over my face. My eyes felt rimmed with pain. She pressed papers into my hand. "Call any of these numbers," she urged. "Whenever you're ready, there are people who can help." She opened the door for us to leave with her.

Paul guided me out through the double doors. A few yards ahead of us, Jack and Margaret sat in the yellow glow of a low lamp. They rose as we approached. Slowly, the corners of their mouths turned up. I looked down at what I was wearing. I looked up and grinned.

MONDAY, MARCH 7

It helps that today is sunny. I'm actually feeling energized this morning. Group Health's mental-health clinic rescheduled my appointment to tomorrow, so today I can concentrate on this week's anxiety: Paul's business trip to Kodiak.

He leaves today at 6:05 P.M. Traveling to construction sites for design reviews is a normal part of his job. I used to enjoy my time alone; now the thought of him out of reach for three days and nights is like having my air supply cut off. The fear I felt yesterday was only, finally, subdued when I planned with Paul when, how, and with whom we would drive to the airport. At first we thought of his sister, but Chris can't easily get away from her carpentry job. Jack will be perfect. He'll make no less and no more of the experience than it will demand, and I will be spending the rest of the evening with him and Margaret anyway. Staying alone at night on *Orca* would be impossible.

I am going to try to motivate myself in Paul's absence to accomplish something on *Orca*. My list so far is modest; surely I can get every one of those tasks done. If I jump in and start, as

I did Saturday with cleaning the walls in the main cabin, I will eventually finish them all. The trick is not to think ahead to the next job and then the next. Thinking ahead seems to paralyze me.

The week seems so opportune: Paul leaves today, Monday, and returns Thursday. Our friends from Juneau, Alice and Scott, arrive on Friday night; they have called regularly since our return from St. Martin, and I am anxious to see them. The four of us will cruise off the next day on *Orca* for a week in the San Juan Islands. Meanwhile, I get things ready. All very tidy. All now unbelievably difficult for me. Time used to be something I could divide up into measured tasks. Now it has become a vast sea in which I float aimlessly.

Slept well again last night. It has been some time now since I have awakened in tears (maybe four whole nights!), though always always the memory awakens with me. And I still wake early and reach for Paul. What will it be like tonight sleeping without him?

Portland, Oregon
March 7, 1988

Migael and Paul,

At times, one needs to lay hands on friends, for reassurance that they still exist and walk the earth. That's what I felt about you two—and now *I* feel better. Migael, it will get better. As one of the walking wounded, I promise you this. Paul, you are and look marvelous. I appreciate anew the loving, teddy-bear quality about you. I know you are taking care of each other.

We'll plan a Portland visit for the spring. I'm always here—always broad-shouldered—always available—and always fascinated by *anything* you have to say.

My love,
Anna

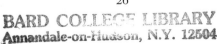

WEDNESDAY, MARCH 9

It was just as hard as I expected, saying good-bye to Paul. For most of the ride out to the airport I was calm and even felt a bit casual, though I caught myself nervously fingering his rolls of architectural drawings as we approached. It wasn't until Jack stopped the car that all my fears exploded. Paul's departure was physically painful; when I finally let go of him and returned to the car it took real effort not to run back after him. Jack summed it up exactly: "Lots of firsts."

I slept well on the couch that evening, fifteen feet away from Jack and Margaret's reassuring presence in the bedroom. So I was in pretty good spirits yesterday when I walked into Group Health's mental-health clinic. The building alone was immediately reassuring. Brick, multistoried, with narrow mullioned windows, even a turret. As I walked through the tiny courtyard toward the arched main doorway I felt as though I was entering a protective castle. But I was nervous as I approached the reception desk, and as I sat in the waiting room. I had never been to a therapist before. Would it work?

The counselor approached, a jangle of keys in her hand. "Migael Scherer?" she asked, pronouncing my name perfectly. "I'm Judy Burns." She was tall and black and perfectly composed.

In her office I sat at the side of her desk. To my left was a round trash can and, close to me on the desktop, a box of tissue. The low lamps and the soft chairs relaxed me. It was easy for me to tell her what had happened, and how I have been feeling since.

"Your reactions make perfect sense to me," she said when I was done. "Disturbing as they are to you, they're perfectly normal."

"Normal?"

"Yes. It's the experience you had that's abnormal."

"So what else is normal?" I asked. "Will I ever get back to

the other 'normal'? Are there stages I can expect to go through?"

"It's not so simple as that," she replied. "There are stages, yes, like those around death: grief, fear, anger, and so on. But there's no certain order. They can overlap, switch around. It's different for every survivor."

"What can I do to make it better?"

"Is there anything you've done already that helps?"

"Well," I said, thinking. "It calms me a lot to talk or write about it. I seem to need to tell the story over and over, or parts of it over and over, and it helps when I can." She nodded, encouraging me to go on. "And being with certain people. That helps me too."

"You feel safe with them," she said.

"Yes, that's it exactly. They make me feel safe. My husband, my really good friends, they're wonderful. They're not afraid to get close to me. Others, I can't even be around. They don't mean to hurt me, I suppose, but they do." I looked down at the carpeted floor. "I wish I could do something about that."

"You don't need to," Judy said. "You're not responsible for anyone's reaction to your assault. If someone's reaction hurts you, it's OK to stay away from them."

"What about someone like my father? How can I ignore *him*?"

"Did his response surprise you?" she asked.

I shook my head. "He's like a lot of fathers, I suppose. All closed up, very disciplined and formal. In fact, he was a career officer in the army."

"So he's never been the kind of father you went to for help?"

"Not this kind of help. I don't mean he's stingy or anything—he's not. But emotion is something he doesn't like to be around." I stopped, reluctant to go further. There was something here that hurt.

Judy shifted slightly in her chair. "Some people have no strengths in this area. They can't express their own feelings, let alone help someone else." She paused, as though reflecting on someone she knew. "It sounds like your father has been taking care of himself for a long time. He can do it now."

"But what if the relationship gets worse because I stay away? Not just him, with others too. Won't I have more work, later?"

"It's not your job to mend the rift, or to educate others about your assault. Remember, you didn't ask to be raped. It's not you who's caused all this turmoil—don't take the blame." Her voice softened. "What's important now is that you take care of yourself."

Everything she said made sense, and helped, but for some reason I expected more. I felt more stirred up than settled. I left not knowing if I would ever see her again.

My sleep on Jack and Margaret's couch last night was broken by one disturbing dream after another. In the last dream I was in a laundromat, loading clothes into two or three washers. I couldn't get the quarters to fit in the horizontal slots (each slot marked with a cartoon), or all the laundry to fit into the machines I had selected. The dirty clothes seemed to multiply. I despaired of ever getting them into the dryers. I would be there forever. I awoke in tears.

In need of companionship today, I took my laundry up to Stan and Teri's. I was soothed by the pulse of their home, cluttered with Teri's paintings, Stan's building projects, and their children's toys. Ben's attempt to help me fold Paul's T-shirts, which are almost as long as Ben is tall, distracted me from my own emptiness. After lunch I helped Teri pack the boys into their carseats. She left for day-care and her office just as Stan returned from working with his own clients.

The two of us read the paper in silence at the dining room table. The last of my laundry was drying in the basement.

"How are you doing, Migael?" Stan asked, cutting through the casual mood I'd been affecting since I'd arrived. "Are you feeling connected to your body these days?"

How had he known to ask that question? "No," I said. "No, I am not." Stan nodded thoughtfully; my answer did not surprise him.

Of course! The sense of my body as separate, almost dangerous, accounts for so much: my feeling translucent, my intense need for physical intimacy, my skewed time sense. I *had* been removed from my body. It never occurred to me that settling back inside myself would be so disturbing.

THURSDAY, MARCH 10

I really lost it last night. It began about 7:30, when I suddenly realized that I had been alone too long. Fearing Margaret wasn't home yet, I called Jack at work, who said he'd slip away and meet me at the house. Racing against my rising panic, I grabbed food for the promised salad, stopped at the deli for chips and a newspaper (I am recently keen on news), and almost made it to the door. Almost.

Halfway down the steps that lead to the house I began gasping and sobbing. I stopped to collect myself, then continued. Through the window in the back door I could see Margaret taking off her jacket and chatting happily on the phone; she must have just arrived. I let myself in, carefully avoiding her gaze, but as soon as she hung up and looked at me I began crying. She put her arms around me. Jack walked in the door, set his briefcase on the floor, and wordlessly embraced us both. Dragged all the way down to those dark moments, I could barely breathe.

"I guess I don't need to explain," I said as I cried. They shook their heads. Gently, Jack and Margaret held me up and held me together.

It seemed like a long time before I disentangled myself from their arms, before the tears stopped falling. Margaret and I made the taco salad, we ate by candlelight, and I got into my nightshirt and under the blanket on the couch. I was limp and relaxed; even my fingers were exhausted. We all fell asleep there, woke at 2:00 A.M., arranged ourselves in our beds, fell asleep again. Though I awoke often, my sleep was deep, dreamless, and completely restful.

SATURDAY, MARCH 12

Paul's return Thursday evening affected me immediately. The instant I saw him walking off the plane, my breathing returned to its normal rate and depth.

And he was so real and full of another life, clearly energized by his adventures in Kodiak. His eyes were so bright they startled me. He held up his carry-on bag to show off the stiff package that protruded from it. "You didn't think I'd come back without a salmon, did you?" he said, throwing his free arm around me. "Even if I had to take it from someone's freezer. Which I did." As we walked to the car and drove home he rattled on about who he'd seen and what he'd done, oblivious (so I thought) to my delight. All I wanted to do was look at him and hold him.

At home aboard *Orca* Paul unwrapped the salmon down to the aluminum foil and lay it in the galley sink to thaw. Almost two feet long without head or tail, it tilted upward over the counter.

"Plenty enough to share," he declared. "Who do you want to have over tomorrow? We haven't seen the Larsons in a long time."

I felt myself close up instantly against a force I couldn't understand. I said nothing.

Paul looked up and saw the confusion in my face. "What's wrong? You're acting like this salmon is some kind of burden or something."

"It's not that . . ." I said.

"Look. I've just come home from Kodiak with a fifteen-pound salmon. What's wrong with wanting to share it?" He raised his voice just slightly. "I want to do something fun and spontaneous around here for a change, and you're giving me a look like I'm some kind of bully."

It was true. My eyes were wide and fixed. What was going on? Always before when he'd been gone for a while there was a brief awkwardness, sure, but this felt different.

31

"Well, I'm not!" he said, his voice louder still. I retreated into the corner of the settee, drew my knees up to my chin. I stared at him in disbelief. My ears roared. "Jesus, Migael!" He sat down on the couch, sighed and rubbed his face, up and down, with both hands. When he finally spoke his voice was soft. "I don't understand. I don't know how to handle this. I don't want to hurt you."

"Please don't hurt me!" I blurted out, and at the same time rushed to sit beside him. He lifted me into his lap, pressed the side of my face against his. Like my own, it was wet with tears.

That night I slept deeply and long. The whole bright next day seemed clear for all the little preparations I wanted to make before Alice and Scott arrived from Juneau late that evening. But I heeded the tug (at Stan's recommendation) to let Detective Peters know I was leaving town for the San Juan Islands. Twenty minutes after I spoke with him another detective, Kelly O'Brien, called to ask if I could give them time today for some detailed questioning. We settled on 10:30, only forty minutes later, aboard *Orca*. I hung up and felt a rush of fear; mindlessly I ironed shirts and put things away.

The detectives arrived in suits, easy smiles on their faces, firm handshakes—clearly comfortable with what they were doing. O'Brien, a little taller, a little leaner than Peters, carried a thick black three-ring binder. Their manner, the beauty of the day, and the security of *Orca* relaxed me as much as was possible under the circumstances.

But it was hard. I told my story twice, the first time— thankfully—without a tape recorder humming in front of me on the galley table. My whole body moved and tensed with each telling. O'Brien's questions were detailed and adept, transporting me back into that laundromat, into that event as both participant and observer. Did he have a watch? Describe his hands. Did I hear a dryer going when I returned from Safeway? Describe the other man who was doing his wash when I first came in. Did his shoes make noise? How many fingers did he put inside me? I remembered clearly details I was unaware I had even noticed. How had he choked me? I clenched O'Brien's upraised wrist with both hands, as though it were my neck.

And as I relived and remembered, the two detectives listened and watched (I'm sure Peters was especially watching me as I spoke to O'Brien's intense face), their thoughts almost visibly shifting, connecting, concluding, and speculating. Occasionally a theory would be expressed: that he was almost surely on foot that morning and probably lives nearby, that he is sexually impotent, that he may have been hunting me down for some time. But the most chilling conclusion was explained at the very end, when I asked the question that has haunted me for over a month. Why had he stopped strangling me?

The detectives exchanged glances across the cabin, then turned back to me.

"He was right when he said you were a lucky woman," O'Brien began. "You *were*. I had to listen to that part twice to believe it." He paused. "As soon as he pulled your shirts over your head, you lost your identity. You became the woman he hates. You were the woman"—he clenched his fist and jerked his right arm—"who jerks his chain. When that happened he was out of control." O'Brien looked at me steadily, as though considering his next words. "Women don't usually survive that."

I shot a questioning look at Peters, who was nodding slowly. "Why did he stop?" I asked, my hands on my neck.

"You scared him," O'Brien answered simply. "When you exhaled you made a sound and went limp. He thought he had killed you, and it scared him."

Incredible news. My life had pivoted on a desperate intuition that I should exhale and calm down. The advice I heard a hundred times in Alaska: In the grip of a bear attack, play dead. The repeated advice in the childbirth manual I edited years ago: Exhale slowly to relax and conserve energy. And my own wild determination to live. I owe my survival to so many others. Perhaps at that instant I really wasn't alone.

3

RENEWAL

Yet still I am loved by the sun, and still am part of earth.

—EDITH SITWELL

MONDAY, MARCH 14

Friday night I slept only three hours. All my dreams centered around my fear and the remoteness of others, especially Paul. When I turned to him in bed he seemed to move away from me, out of reach. My final waking was agonized and tearful. Opening my soul and then my body to him, I at last began to regain my balance, my buoyancy.

I felt sheltered and connected, but still fragile and transparent all day until we prepared to leave. Paul turned on the engine, and *Orca* was magically transformed from a floating home to a cruising sailboat. I directed Scott and Alice as we stowed gear, latched drawers, pulled out charts and tide tables and binoculars. Paul opened the log on the chart table, turned on the VHF radio and the depth-sounder. We collapsed the cockpit awning and rearranged fenders. At Paul's signal from the helm we tossed the lines on to the dock.

Heading for the Ballard Locks in the bright afternoon, all my tension evaporated. The motions of tossing and tending lines as we were lowered into Puget Sound energized me in a way I had not felt for months. The freshwater smell gave way to salt, and I realized with pleasure that the terror had retreated. I felt instantly rested, nourished, able-bodied, and strong. At anchor in Port Madison I slept seven hours, my longest sleep since those final nights in St. Martin. Noting the change in me, Alice remarked that perhaps I should cruise for the rest of my life. It's a pretty tempting thought. Though I am physically not far from Seattle, I am emotionally distanced. What a release!

Scott and Alice are perfect cruising companions. We had been together last in Glacier Bay, where they had flown to meet us in Alice's little Cessna. The easy days pulling crab pots and hiking the empty trails had been a perfect way of saying good-bye to them, and to Alaska, last summer. Now it is as though they had made the trip south with us, as though we had never been apart. I feel free to say whatever comes to mind about my feelings, whenever it comes to mind. They exude calmness.

Sunday was easy and happy. We all woke up when we wanted, moved at a pace governed only by our readiness to flow into the next activity. As always in cruising, time and tide and weather are the major factors, and yesterday they were on our side. Even gave us some clamming time south of the Port Townsend Canal. In the light rain, while Scott and I perhaps dug too much for too few clams, *Orca* floated offshore in the pale-pink, blue-gray light.

My only tension developed when Helen and Brad, sailing friends we hadn't seen since last fall, met the four of us at the tavern in Port Townsend. I had called them from a pay phone, hoping we could get together alone the next morning. Brad suggested he and Helen meet us that night as well. "We're just sitting at home," he said. "We'd love to see you."

They joined us at the large round table, smiled at Scott and

Alice as Paul introduced them. I poured beer for the two of them from the heavy glass pitcher. Brad pulled off his cap and scratched his red beard. I could feel him searching my face, trying to catch my eyes as they avoided his.

"So what's been up with you two?" he asked, directing his question at me. He was smiling, but his eyes were not.

I looked quickly at Paul and Scott and Alice, as though I expected them to answer. It's OK, their faces told me. Go ahead, if you want.

"It's bad," I said, and put the pitcher down. "Last month . . . I was raped. In the middle of the morning. In a laundromat in Ballard."

Helen's eyes darkened instantly, like a black mirror. Brad sighed and took a deep drink from his beer. "Thanks for telling me now," he said after he set down his glass. "I heard something in your voice on the phone and wanted to see you right away. Thanks." He took another drink, and the tension dissolved.

The topic was gently set aside for the rest of the evening. But promptly at seven this morning it was opened again over coffee in the Salal Café. Brad and Helen ate breakfast—oatmeal—but I can't remember even seeing their bowls arrive. "Tell us all about it," Brad said, his eyes bright, ready.

By now I should be skilled at telling my story, but I still tumble over phrases, wet my lips. I am clearly still in its grip. As are my listeners, the ones who count, at any rate. The ones who feel with me.

Outside the café Brad held me tightly. Helen embraced me in a soft sway.

"It's going to be hard for you guys to teach this morning," I said.

"Don't worry about us," Helen said. "Those kids will take one look at our faces and know we mean business. You have a wonderful cruise. We'll be in touch." They waved good-bye from Brad's truck. We headed back to *Orca* and pushed off.

WEDNESDAY, MARCH 16

Another Tuesday has come and gone. Just before 10:00 A.M. half a dozen porpoises joined us as we crossed Haro Strait into Canada. Their speed and beauty as they crisscrossed our bow made us all laugh. And I thought: That is what I must become to evade the shark. Something fast and full of fun. Something very alive.

The elation of the porpoises' visit was followed in the next half hour by my emotional withdrawal. I sat next to Scott behind the pilothouse, my hand on his shoulder, sheltered from the wind. Paul came on deck and I moved to his seat in the cockpit, wrapped my arms around his legs. It was the longest half hour of the week. Someday I will not even remember it, but yesterday, though surrounded by friends and sun and water and *Orca's* reassuring motion, that half hour was immobilizing.

After clearing Canadian customs in Victoria we tied up in front of the Empress Hotel, sipped beers in a café on the seawall, squinted in the sun. We lucked out and got a table at the Empress for afternoon tea. The time was right for the cloying sweetness of biscuits, clotted cream, jam, and scones. We ventured up the main street to shop, Scott and Paul for cigars, Alice for new sweatpants. All of us are adopting the faraway gaze and easy pace of cruising.

Scott christened this "Migael Day," and pointed to the cannon prepared for a salute (intended actually for the king and queen of Sweden in town for the opening of Parliament), the ranks forming for a parade, the new blossoms on the trees. Spring was unfolding before us, all its sweet smells and colors insisting on being noticed. And the weather forecast: sunshine everywhere.

We are fast approaching Sucia Island, where we intend to spend the next two nights. I just finished embroidering my emergency-room bathrobe, transforming the Property of

Consolidated Hospital Supply logo into a life ring that surrounds the red sails of a ketch, a satisfying task that made me feel renewed. I have a strong urge to wear it all the time.

I have slept long and well four nights in a row. And what a treat to wake up, fully rested, into bright sunshine each morning.

THURSDAY, MARCH 17

I awoke in the middle of the night from an erotic dream. Before the dark memories could settle in (that face is always waiting in my first waking moments) I reached for Paul, who was eager and ready. As I am so often now. Never has my desire for him been so easily aroused. Making love has achieved a prominence I never would have expected after nineteen years of marriage. Of course, lovemaking recalls the rape to me, and I occasionally become lost in a flashback. But it always subsides, driven out by desire, pleasure, and love. Then it was pain and terror, all foreplay leading to strangling and oblivion. Now all the emotions and sensations are soft and open, and the oblivion of orgasm is more powerful than the violence. Often, I am moved to tears.

Some days I have only two emotions: cold terror (abrupt, jagged) and warm desire (soft, pulsing).

And the world seems in tune with me. As the four of us walked all over Sucia Island everything was new, fecund. New leaves, the pink buds of new cones, bright grass on the trail, sweet warming damp soil. Even the crabs are locked together. (This particular event was later revealed to be a large crab eating a much smaller crab; so much for life-affirming symbols.)

We have given over the day entirely to whim and pleasure. Alice and Scott do not even look like the same people we picked up at the airport last Friday. Their faces are gently browned, their eyes relaxed, their smiles wide. Alice's hair falls loosely from her baseball cap; Scott's smooth face has turned to stubble. I imagine Paul and I look different as well. What powerful restorative medicine cruising is.

SATURDAY, MARCH 19

I have been mulling over the subject of safety and backup systems, and this morning's Coast Guard inspection in Guemes Channel seems like a clear enough sign that I should give this some attention. The young, bright-eyed Coasties flashed tentative smiles as they boarded *Orca*. We passed, of course, with no violations.

And why should we be anxious? We have built and equipped our boat with every safety device we can afford. Her bow has a collision bulkhead. Every compartment has a fire extinguisher, and the engine room its own system. We have float-coats with strobe lights, life rings, life jackets, and an overboard pole with strobe. Sails, a diesel engine, and a gasoline kicker. Two dinghies and a life raft. Enough tools to rebuild practically the entire boat. Under way I feel prepared, ready for danger.

So when is my life in greatest peril? When I am entirely relaxed, distracted by the familiar task of sorting wet laundry in a familiar laundromat, feeling on top of things. I had that morning, after all, a good start on the day, even the beginning of a letter to a friend, and had prepared myself for the only inconvenience I anticipated—a shortage of quarters for the laundry machines.

I did not even sense the circling shark. What was there to be afraid of? I saw only a quiet man of average build sitting, legs crossed, reading away his laundry cycles.

And what, when he struck, could I have used to defend myself and survive? I reached for the obvious: physical strength (what did I know about fighting a man already in control with a knife?), bargaining (why should he have cared about money while gripped by his own obsession?), even my will (again, a blade at the throat, and pain and blood, are compelling arguments). All I had left were my wits, my forty years of life experience, which fortunately included controlling my own fear (though never ever this kind of fear), taking responsibility for myself, pushing through a sense of helplessness. Of course, he very nearly prevailed. I never gained the upper hand on his dark frenzy. If anything, his encounter with me whetted rather than sated his need to control and hurt. But I survived, without a life ring or even a lookout. With luck and the systems at hand.

MONDAY, MARCH 21

Scott and Alice are well on their way back to Juneau. Paul and I are back in Seattle, have eaten our leftover lasagna dinner, read and sorted the mail (which included several touching notes from dear friends), and have settled into some quiet evening tasks. *Orca* seems so empty now; all the liveliness of friends and new sights is gone. I am feeling a bit empty myself. It is time to return to everyday living, no less or more "real" than the past week.

After this past week I can point to some real progress. For one, I finally feel rested, more connected with my physical surroundings, my own body, even the feelings and concerns of others. I have almost lost the sense of aimless drifting. For one week I have had the experience of making decisions, taking care of others, handling sails and lines. Tied to the dock in Ballard again I am ready to control my drift in time and space.

I'm not foolish enough to believe this sense of control will last. After all, it has taken over a month and two outstanding vacations to bring me to this point. And I was reminded of my fragility on Saturday, when the return to Seattle was imminent and the fear came back. Here I am, it said, as powerful as ever. Today, driving Scott and Alice to the airport, the familiar fatigue behind my eyes returned. Already I was more tense and watchful, scanning faces for that one face, jumping at the morning phone ring.

WEDNESDAY, MARCH 23

Why does Tuesday continue to be so hard? I don't want it to be. I try to forget that I was attacked on a Tuesday. Yesterday I began with my to-do list, determined to make this one different. Everything got jumbled. I called Detective Peters to pass on a hunch about my attacker's eye color, the possibility that he was wearing contact lenses, and another detail I remembered: When I entered the laundromat, he was sitting in a white metal chair. I hadn't seen those chairs in many months. In exchange for my information, I learned that my taped statement had been inadvertently erased. The specter of another detailed retelling loomed large and definite.

At 10:00 A.M. I headed for the bank. Time crawling as it does on Tuesday morning, at 10:25 I turned toward Margaret's office. Engrossed in balance sheets and ledgers, working against a deadline, she barely acknowledged my presence. Wrong place, I thought to myself, baffled by the strangeness of normal life. Sinking fast, I turned to leave. But Margaret heard the appeal in my voice and caught me as I was turning the doorknob; her hug saved me from drowning altogether.

An hour, a cup of coffee, some conversation, and I was back on course. But I had been weakened, and despite the fact that I got *Orca* all cleaned up inside and made all the calls I wanted, I never did regain a full sense of control. Only later that evening, talking with Paul about those final moments in the grip of those choking hands, was I able to truly come to the surface.

Today has been much better. My very best day alone, as a matter of fact. Almost everything that happened was at my own initiative. Did laundry at Stan and Teri's, shopped for groceries at the Safeway near the laundromat with only minor anxieties, even drove by the laundromat (only the quickest of glances, but I saw two men blithely washing clothes). Read the paper, scrubbed the main cabin and pilothouse floors, started and finished a letter. Walked all the way into downtown Ballard and back for the *News-Tribune*. Of course I was jumpy and stretched. Scanning every face and avoiding perceived traps takes a lot of energy. But I also feel a childish sense of accomplishment.

Which I hope to carry over into tomorrow. While straightening up the pilothouse today I ran across the teacher-placement files and application forms I had filled out during the weeks before February 9. Crisply typed and paper clipped, they had been forgotten behind the compass all this time. I paged through them slowly, dimly recalling my energetic plans to find work this winter. The prospect of teaching that charged me then overwhelms me now; I haven't the heart to submit the applications. Or the need; the counselor I spoke with at Group Health, my friends, and Paul, all encourage me to take care of myself at this time. Wait until it feels right to look for work, they say. I am grateful for the freedom Paul's steady job provides. Still, the pile of papers tugs at me. Part of it, the placement file, is a piece I can complete now. It's all ready, all the transcript information updated, all my recommendations in order. All that's required is to mail it in, something I think I can do tomorrow. I won't be committing myself to anything, just leaving the door open should I decide to teach later. It seems such a small gesture, given all my efforts two months ago, when finding a job seemed so important.

FRIDAY, MARCH 25

I am almost immobilized by fear today. My breathing is shallow, my heart constricted. I am obsessed with entrapment fantasies in which I am the predator and the sandy-haired, innocuous-looking rapist is the unwitting prey. In those fantasies—they are almost dreams—I cannot convince anyone to help me because he looks so harmless. The only way I can get help is when he turns back into the predator and I am under attack again, sometimes under his hands, sometimes under his knife, which stabs rather than slices.

And yesterday was so good. Who knows what turned it around, or will turn it around again? My father's phone call earlier this morning announcing that he and my mother would be over only increased my confused fear. (Why, why can't he *ask*, give up his need to be in charge for just a little while?) During their brief visit I sat stiffly in the main cabin, struggling to follow his remarks about the book he was returning. The intellectual banter that used to characterize our conversation exhausted me. I held back the helplessness I felt as we talked. I pretended to be all right. So much of my life has been spent, I now realize, trying to show him I am strong and grown up. I know I have been avoiding my father, and feel guilty despite the professional advice not to. My sister's call from Juneau helped; Gloria confessed to feeling the same need to withdraw when her son became mentally ill last fall. Her words eased my guilt, but the helplessness remains.

MONDAY, MARCH 28

Frustrated by the physical distance between us and what she described as an intense need to hold me in her arms, Debra flew down from Juneau last weekend. Like Scott and Alice, Debra is a relatively new friend—four years ago we did not know each other. A love of halibut fishing had brought us together. How many hours we had spent in her small boat, jigging our baited hooks, squinting toward Admiralty Island, listening (one magical day) to humpback whales groan and splash in the channel. I am touched by her eagerness to be with me now.

We had some fun times with her friends, a beautiful drive to Poulsbo, a dizzying shopping trip in downtown Seattle. I followed her energetic, pony-tailed form as she trolled through department stores, picking out a dress here, a perfume there, and fresh chocolate—her favorite—to share with Paul. Through all our wanderings, we talked. It felt good to tell my story to her, often and in many different ways. What I appreciated most was her anger. Debra is so angry that she refuses to acknowledge any good that is emerging from my attack. And she is so eloquent in her anger—perhaps being an attorney has given her lots of practice—that she has pried open a little of my own.

WEDNESDAY, MARCH 30

Ha! I'd clearly forgotten what it really felt like to be afraid until this morning. What was intended to be a simple breakfast at Lambert's with Paul, who will be gone on business overnight to San Francisco, was instead thirty minutes of high tension. All because of a man who vaguely resembled "my" rapist.

Probably what triggered it was that he was reading a newspaper. The set of his shoulders and the part of his hair, his short nose and his cheekbones and even his forehead were almost the same. The effect was so overwhelming I could barely sip my coffee.

But he was not the same man. His hair was too thin and too receding. His eyes were brown and a little too small for his face, which was a little too full. And his complexion was too coarse, as though he'd had acne when he was young. Despite these very clear differences, when he put on his blue-gray jacket and walked toward us at the counter to pay his bill I could hear my heart's roar. And I could not resist watching him walk across the street and drive off in his silver-colored car.

So that is what it will be like if I ever do see the man who attacked me seven weeks ago. I have been given a sort of rehearsal. I will need to make certain that it is he as quickly as possible. I will need to move and act immediately and ignore the strong urge to do nothing. It will take more strength than I would have imagined.

Paul, of course, was aware of my distress, and did what he could to diffuse it. The glass of water was the best, and his steadiness. Leaving him in front of his office building wasn't even excruciatingly difficult, only mildly so. And he has not left for San Francisco yet. He is still downtown, working as usual. Will I know it when his plane lifts off at 1:30 this afternoon? Will my breathing change as it did during his last absence?

Later in the morning Detective O'Brien arrived for a retape of my statement. The session was easier than anticipated.

"He's going to be hard to catch, isn't he?" I said after O'Brien had turned off the tape recorder.

"He doesn't leave anything behind," O'Brien agreed. "No sperm, nothing. This guy's so pathetic he can't even get it up."

"Well," I said, "that doesn't make him less dangerous."

O'Brien looked at me sharply. "He didn't set out to kill you," he told me, as though he had read my thoughts. "He may have been as scared as you were when he realized what he was doing." A brief, heavy silence lay between us. "Have you told anyone else about all this?"

"I've told everyone," I replied. "Everyone."

"Good," he said, closing his three-ring binder, preparing to leave. "It's good you're taking care of yourself that way. When it comes to nailing this guy, you're one of the best witnesses we've got."

4

QUICKSAND
FEELINGS

I am terrified by this dark thing
That sleeps in me:
All day long I feel its soft, feathery turnings, its
*   malignity.*

—Sylvia Plath

FRIDAY, APRIL 1

Paul was out of town only one night. It was better this time. I arranged to stay with Margaret and Jack. And Margaret, remembering my breakdown last month when Paul was in Kodiak, had arranged for me to join her Wednesday-evening yoga class. "We're all beginners," she explained when she invited me. "There's no real pressure. It helps me a lot. Maybe it'll work for you."

It did. The quiet pace of the yoga positions wrung out every muscle I have. The hour and a half of activity was a refreshing change from my general passivity these past months. At last I was throwing my body into something challenging, something that required effort but would not hurt it.

At Jack and Margaret's afterward I felt as though I'd been massaged all over. But I was not truly relaxed. The adrenaline rush of the morning, when I thought I'd seen "him," the retape of my statement with O'Brien, and the fact that I started my period in the afternoon—all these events confused the pleasurable results from the yoga. Curled against Jack on the couch, stroking the cat's purring, silky body, I wept silently. Jack gently stroked my hair and face, moving the fear and sadness aside. Margaret roused herself from the corner of the couch where she had dozed off and we all wordlessly settled into our beds. Throughout the night I woke often, but generally slept well. Though I missed Paul, I was filled with love and gratitude for these dear friends.

MONDAY, APRIL 4

Yesterday was so gloriously enjoyable that I could almost snub the dark memories. When they tugged at my sleeve I was able to say, "Beat it. I'm having too much fun. Leave me alone." And for the most part the memories obeyed—through coffee and the Sunday paper at the Salmon Bay Café, through champagne and the Easter-egg hunt and brunch at Stan and Teri's. During our walk in the long, light evening Paul and I glanced into the golden interiors of tidy Ballard homes. I felt balanced and on the verge of learning how to integrate those twenty minutes with years of peacefulness and happiness.

Of course, the memories reasserted themselves. First, as I was relaxing into sleep and later, having failed to hold my attention long enough, in my dreams. I really haven't had many nightmares. My worst one, in which I witness my own rape and strangling from the periphery of a crowded, swaying dance floor, occurred many weeks ago in the Caribbean. Last night's nightmare was an embellishment of the one I had the

Friday Scott and Alice arrived, before we went cruising. Once again, the sky exploded. It exploded from below (though not from the earth) with geysers of inky, oily blackness. No one seemed alarmed; it had been anticipated and even prepared for. As the blackness intensified, fully visible through huge plate-glass windows, people descended into the ground in glass-enclosed elevators that I (alone?) was unable to board. I watched one small brown-haired woman descend and wanted to protect her. Was she me? I looked hopelessly at the sun, which was obscured by shifting, thickening black mist. I awoke.

It was dark, and 3:30, and too warm under the flannel sheet and quilts. I was dazed and damp with sweat. The wind gusted through the rigging. Afraid to retreat into my dream, I cast about for a safe thought or memory. The shark muscled them aside. I wrapped myself around Paul and focused on the security of his body, the safe strength of his arms. The shark took firm hold of my heart and dove deep. And there I was for the next three hours, trapped in the Kwik-Kleen laundromat, alternately immobilized by gripping, caressing, strangling hands. I reviewed every word, every flinch, every action. I memorized the sound of his voice, his posture, every detail of his face. Could I have noticed more? Should I have kept my eyes wide open? Could I have escaped? I jumped around through the event, never able to move from beginning to end, searching for a way out.

The sound of the clock radio brought me gasping to the surface. I was able to doze after Paul left for work, but my dreams were still troubling. In an imagined bathroom in the laundromat I tried to put on huge, stiff, cloudy contact lenses, while my attacker patiently waited and advised. I slipped naked from a bed and into a feathered robe while he watched and then approached, similarly costumed.

When I awoke, I lay in bed staring at the cedar overhead, watching the sun dapple the walls. How I miss myself, the me I used to be. How I miss the confident Migael who lay in the same bed the morning of February 9 and thought: OK, let's see. Laundry first, and a little grocery shopping, then get all my packing done. Get that letter off to Debra and boy oh boy we're going to have fun in St. Martin. I miss my enthusiasm and physical energy. I miss my eagerness to help others. I miss my innocence. All changed.

TUESDAY, APRIL 5

David's letter arrived yesterday. As ever since our college days, he makes me think in new ways. I keep reading his letter, over and over. I cannot put it down.

Anchorage, Alaska
April 1988

Dear Migael,
   A few weeks ago Paul told me about your terrible experience of February 9. When I spoke to him of writing to you, I think I wanted mostly to express dismay and hope and to join, if only from a distance, every force tending toward your healing.
   An experience of mine may or may not be of help. For a few days in 1978 I believed that I had lymphatic cancer. I will spare you a description of the emotional topography of the crisis itself. You may find more interest in what happened after it was over.
   Of course, I was elated when the doctors said that I didn't have cancer. Within a few days, however, I became aware that my feelings were not returning to "normal." I alternated between relief, on the one hand, and confusion and even depression, on the other. Although there was no objective reason I couldn't carry on with the plans I had made before the crisis (parenthood, law school), question marks seemed to hang over everything. The crisis itself pointed to no particular direction, made no decisions for me.

Perversely, it seemed only to have drained the decisions
I had made before it of emotional satisfaction.

My feelings of confusion were worse when I tried to
explain how I felt to other people. Elsa, who was
pregnant and suffered greatly through the whole thing,
simply shut the subject out, didn't want to hear about it
(for which I didn't, and don't, blame her). A close
friend kept saying, "Well, you're all right, that's all that
matters"; he was incapable of grasping that *the fear was as
important as the relief,* that the fear itself had a fascination
and a quickening power.

I don't know whether you feel anything like what I
describe. But if you do, the best advice I can give you is
to observe, but do not trust, your feelings at this stage.
They are like quicksand, deceptive and unstable. They
may lead you to make demands on yourself which will
not only be unfair and increase your confusion, but
which may actually obscure from you the real, abiding
meaning of the experience itself.

My post-traumatic feelings did, of course, eventually
pass away. It was surprisingly long before they did,
about three months. And it was more than a year before
I realized I no longer had a fearful anticipation of death.
I had acquired, unexpectedly, a kind of coolness about
death, but it was more a lack of concern than a swagger,
a willingness to let death come in its own time and
manner and to live without unnecessary and useless
anxiety about it. The change I felt should result from
the experience had occurred, but it was subtler than I
knew how to look for.

So, perhaps, it will be for you. I think whatever
meanings these events have, they themselves will
disclose over time. Beware of trying to make a meaning
for them.

I hope, Migael, I haven't presumed too much in
saying anything. Our culture doesn't seem to have a

standard way to express *respect* for another's suffering, except by silence. (In Asia, you can bow to the person.) I didn't want to keep silent about this; you should know your friends are with you.

David

WEDNESDAY, APRIL 6

I spent yesterday almost entirely with Paul's sister. Since the Thursday after the attack, when Chris took time off work to care for me, she has been a spirited, steady support. Now she is caught up in the excitement of preparing for her three-month trip to Europe, and I in the anxiety over her departure next week.

We began with breakfast at Lambert's, sitting across from each other with our elbows on the yellow Formica table, holding cups of hot coffee with both hands. Her short dark curls framed her face in a tight nap, like Paul's, without the gray. "I'm going to miss you, Migael," Chris said. "Our time together these last two months has meant a lot to me. Especially the breakfasts." She grinned and stuffed a forkful of fried potatoes into her mouth. "Who's going to feed you while I'm gone?" Chris had been bringing us meals almost once a week, which she and Paul, in true Scherer family fashion, would eat hungrily. I would eat what I could, never very much; the weight I had lost since February was noticeable and alarming.

"It's not your food I'm going to miss," I said. I kept my eyes on my plate, determined not to start crying. Not that Chris would mind. She understands my tears, just as she understands that I must describe what happened over and over again to ease an otherwise unbearable pressure.

We took a long walk after breakfast, up Ballard Avenue, along Market Street. I love walking next to Chris, her tall, strong body like a shield. "There's a phone booth right there," she will say, fully aware that I am walking in fear. "If you see him, we'll duck in there and call the cops." Or, sometimes: "Look, if he should walk around the corner right now, that shop's open. We'll be safe." More vigilant than wary. A woman with plans.

"Maybe I'll be better by the time you get back," I said as we headed toward the marina. "Three months is a long time."

"Do you believe that?" Chris asked. "Do you feel like you're making progress?"

"No," I answered. "For a little while I did. But now I feel stalled. I want to move ahead, but I can't. I'm all tangled up. Tired."

"Maybe," Chris offered, "you've gone as far as you can by yourself." No blatant advice. No insistence that I talk to a counselor. Just this simple observation. How I will miss her.

Today I broached the subject with Teri as we folded laundry on her living-room floor. The clothes she pulled from her basket, Jason's footed sleepers and Ben's snap-together pajamas, made me smile. Even when they were at day-care the boys were present.

"What do you tell your clients," I asked, "when they want to know how long it takes to recover from something like I've been through?"

Teri answered immediately, confidently. "I tell them the truth. It takes as long as it takes. A trauma such as yours, Migael, is like a physical wound. You and all the rest of us can do a lot to promote recovery, but no one can hurry it." Teri's words mingled with Chris's, and with those of David's letter. The messages are clear: I am seriously injured. I will heal at my own pace, in my own way.

In yoga class this evening I relished the concentration, the sense of control, the relaxation, even the ache of it. At all times it seemed that when I exhaled or breathed softly I could hold the pose longer, move more gracefully, feel stronger. Margaret has introduced me to a powerful therapy.

TUESDAY, APRIL 12

I find myself these days avoiding something I feel compelled to do in order to move on: to write the physical and emotional details of February 9. I feel that if I do so, for myself alone, I will be able to control the flashbacks a little better, to let go of that day. If I cannot loosen its grip on me, at least I can loosen my grip on it.

Ever since my conversations with Chris and Teri last week, I had been thinking about calling Seattle Rape Relief. The yellow piece of paper given to me in the police station described it as a source of free counseling and information. Judy Burns, the therapist I had seen last month at Group Health, had suggested I give them a try. But for some reason I couldn't bring myself to dial the number. I think it was gentle pressure from Margaret that finally did it. Like Chris, she has been in touch with Rape Relief since my attack, for herself as much as me, she explains. Or perhaps what did it was the alarming pressure I felt when I sat on a white metal chair outside the Quintana Roo restaurant. That chair, a twin of the one I was raped and strangled in, rushed the fear to the surface; my appetite deserted me mid-meal and sleep deserted me at 12:30 that night. (Oh damn, I thought, as I lay awake for hours, envying Paul his deep, even breathing while I tumbled through laundromat reruns and entrapment fantasies, until I settled on one wild idea—that he is a mail carrier in the area—and could catch some sleep about 4:00 A.M.) Exhausted and vulnerable, I called Rape Relief during my morning tea.

I was immediately relieved that I made the call. "Would you like to speak with a counselor?" the woman asked, not waiting for me to phrase my need. And once again I was lucky. Connie Tipton is forty-five, lived on a boat for six years in California, seemed to pick up on the kind of person I am. She did a lot of the talking, reassuring me that I'd done splendidly so far, congratulating me on making the call, assuring me that all my hesitations and confusion, the stalled feelings and grief were not only normal but should be acute at this stage. "After all," she said, "it's only been two months."

"The memories are so vivid," I said. "Are they always going to be like this? In technicolor and full stereo?"

"I know it's hard to believe now," she said, "but they'll fade, with time. That doesn't mean you need to stop talking about what happened, or your feelings. Talking like this is one of the best things you can do to heal."

I was on the phone with Connie for an hour and a half, and needed every minute. She is the first person to tell me that eventually I will be very close to myself again. My former carefree approach to life will of course be tempered by knowledge of what the world really is. Some things are permanently changed. But much of myself will be the same. In time, the Migael I now miss so much will come back.

"I wish I knew when," I sighed. "For some reason I feel like it should all be over in six months. Are you sure there's no shortcut?"

"No shortcuts," she said, "but you can practice being yourself again, if you're up for it. Do something for your own pleasure. Spend a little time with people who know nothing of what happened just for the escape."

Today I took Connie's advice and drove to the high school where I used to teach in order to hear a former student speak about her newly published book. I was flattered that Laura invited me, and proud when I saw what a composed, bright woman she has become. Her decision to write a book about her return to Africa, she said, came after the death of a young friend; she realized that life is too short to put off important goals. As I listened and enjoyed (and later talked with her) I was touched by a lovely reversal: In this same building eight years ago Laura looked to me as a mentor, absorbed my strong energy. Today I was the suggestible, open soul, and she the one full of hope and encouragement.

5

THE VIOLENCE

About suffering they were never wrong,
The Old Masters: how well they understood
Its human position, how it takes place
While someone else is eating or opening a window
or just walking dully along.

—W. H. AUDEN

WEDNESDAY, APRIL 13

OK. Here goes. The events of that Tuesday, February 9, 1988:

I don't remember if I went back to sleep after Paul wiggled my toes good-bye and left for work. But I clearly remember looking up at the cedar overhead and looking ahead to a day full of purpose. Though I had already begun to pack for our vacation (only two more days away!), I had a letter or two to write and a job application to fill out.

But first, the laundry. No big deal; I'd gotten that task down to an hour and a half lately and could squeeze in grocery shopping during the wash cycle. I buzzed through my brief exercise routine (toe touches, sit-ups, press-ups), showered, dressed. It was cold and blustery outside, so at the last moment I put on my striped oxford shirt over my T-shirt and under my sweatshirt.

It was raining when I hauled my blue laundry basket out of the boat. As I started the car I remembered that I needed a roll of quarters. Since it was only nine o'clock and the banks in Ballard don't open until 9:30, I turned left at Shilshole and headed up Leary Way. I'll have a cup of coffee at Lombardi's, I thought, and write to Debra while I wait.

I parked behind the bank and crossed the street to Lombardi's, already composing Debra's letter in my head. I sat at a small table, my back to the window. To my right a woman pored over a stack of legal papers while eating a huge cinnamon roll with her breakfast. Seeing those papers, I thought of the legal briefs piled everywhere in Debra's Juneau office: on her desk, her chairs, even on the floor. I smiled and began writing my letter.

I can't remember exactly what I wrote. It was full of excitement about our upcoming vacation, our new moorage in Ballard, my current job search. I might have made it to the bottom of the sheet when I noticed it was 9:30, closed the tablet, put it in my purse and left, leaving a dollar on the table for the coffee.

It had stopped raining, but the wind had picked up, blowing in gray clouds, white clouds, sometimes allowing the sun to shine through. I could feel the caffeine rush and my slightly empty stomach, but promised myself a real lunch when I returned home. After buying ten dollars' worth of quarters I drove north, then east. As always, traffic was thin. When I passed Ballard High School I reflected on my teaching days and on the applications I had been filling out over the past two weeks. Teaching had been satisfying work, and I would happily return.

There was a parking spot immediately in front of the Kwik-Kleen, so I turned around at the dumpster behind the laundromat, glancing at the blank, barred windows there. I parked, grabbed my basket from the back of the car, and hefted it through the door.

Two men were there that morning, and both were in the aisle of washers and dryers that begins at the door. The man closest to me was working between a washer and dryer. He appeared to be emptying the washing machine, though the dryer behind him was running. Perhaps he was folding dried laundry on top of the washers. He had dark curly hair, dark stubble on his face, and appeared tall to me. A white T-shirt covered his pot belly. He looked up when I came through the door, an open but impersonal look on his face. I seem to remember his voice, appropriately low and gravelly, whether talking to the other man or to himself I don't know. I sensed that they had been talking to each other, or that my arrival had interrupted something, though the demeanor of the second man did not confirm this.

He was sitting in the far corner, just to the left of the two utility doors, in right profile. What caught my eye was the white metal chair he was sitting in. I had not seen one of those chairs in months, and had missed them. I had grown accustomed to sitting on the bench next to the laundry table, but it was awkward. Good, I thought, it will be more comfortable this time if that chair is empty when I return.

His legs were crossed (left over right, I think) and he was reading. His hair was brownish blond, straight, full, combed from a part on his left. A pretty nice haircut. He was slender and what I consider average height. At least so he seemed in his seated position. He did not look up.

I took my laundry to the two front-load washing machines closest to the door, which face the second aisle. Loading them was routine: darks in one, lights in the other. I even threw in the mold-stained green-and-white painter line for our dinghy, something I'd been meaning to wash for weeks. When I poured in the detergent I noticed that my old plastic bottle had finally cracked. I grimaced in annoyance and looked across the washing machines at the two men, both of whom were preoccupied though peripherally aware of me.

My departure for the grocery store would have been uneventful but for the wind. When I opened the door the wind caught it and slammed it loudly against the outside wall. Both men turned toward me. My eyes met for an instant with those of the seated man. He looked at me with his chin down, from under his brows and bangs, his lips parted slightly. I tossed my head, smiled. "Whoa. Lot of wind!" I said as I shifted my basket to my left hip and reached to close the door with my right hand. The black-haired man shrugged and returned my smile. The other did not.

Though I didn't intend to buy much, I drove to the Safeway across the street because the weather was so unsettled. My shopping was simple and quick. Got a little hung up on the Dollar Days sale piles, from which I selected a red dustpan and some scrubbing pads for future boat work.

I don't know what time I returned to the Kwik-Kleen, but when I did the wash cycle wasn't over yet. The black-haired man was gone. The other man had moved to the bench facing my churning wash. He was still reading—a folded newspaper which he held in his left hand. He was seated up against the table, his right elbow resting on the bench arm or, more precisely, I think, on the table itself. I sat down on the bench perpendicular to his, where I could still monitor my wash. I studied him briefly as I pulled the letter to Debra from my purse.

Now I could see him from his left profile. His hairline was about like mine, but with hair much thicker and better-looking. He was wearing a blue-gray jacket, unzipped, with (I think) gathered or ribbed cuffs over a plaid or windowpane cotton shirt whose predominant color was white. He had on jeans and, though I didn't note them specifically, the expected nondescript athletic shoes. He seemed entirely relaxed and engrossed in his reading, totally uninterested in me certainly. To my knowledge he never glanced in my direction. On the whole my impression was of a trim, quiet man in his thirties, perhaps as old as forty. Unalarmed, I turned to my letter, reading over what I'd written so far, adding another sentence or two. The sun was warming my back and lighting the entire room.

The front-load washers always clunk when their cycle is over, so I looked up almost as soon as the red light went off. I tucked my pad and pen into my purse and in one motion stood up, pulled off my jacket, walked the few steps to the washers, and placed my purse and jacket on top of them. I walked in front of the still-reading man to pull a wheeled basket from under the table next to him, pushed it in front of my wash, and emptied the wet laundry into it. I then pushed the basket to the back of the laundromat, where my favorite hot dryers are located.

Just as I was about to load the dryers I thought to go retrieve my purse and jacket from the top of the washers. Although the man didn't strike me as a thief, it seemed the safe thing to do. As I walked toward the washers I glanced at him again. He hadn't moved or changed expression. In contrast, all my actions were quick, decisive, automatic. I was on a roll.

Depositing my coat and purse on the table next to the dryers, I proceeded to load my wet laundry into three of them. I followed my usual procedure: two for jeans, towels, underwear, and T-shirts; one for light shirts and easy-to-dry stuff. I set aside the painter line that I did not want to dry. I thought about our vacation as I tossed in shorts and Paul's white pants, which I had bought the day before.

The smell of a freshly lit cigarette caused me to look quickly over my left shoulder. It is not a smell that belongs with laundered clothes, and it jarred me from my routine. Two or three dryers down the sandy-haired man was staring into a dryer, his right hand on its open door, a filtered cigarette hanging in his mouth. I had not heard him move from the bench, but I hadn't been listening either. I noted his hair, his short, slightly upturned nose, his clean chin line, his well-shaped hand, the color of his jacket. And I noticed that his face had hardened or tensed slightly, as if the cigarette had toughened him.

I turned immediately back to my task and thought to myself: If I wanted to be a jerk I'd ask him to smoke outside. But who really cares? With thoughts of tolerance toward us both I drifted back into the last of my laundry sorting.

It was then that he struck: a tight grip around my ribs, another at my right shoulder and across my neck. Both my hands instantly reached for my throat to pull his hand away. I thought and said, "Jesus, I don't believe this." I felt a cool, sharp hardness pressing across the left side of my neck and thought, Oh, god, a knife. Every alarm inside me was screaming escape. I pulled at his arm, struggled and twisted. I made no sound.

Either as a result of our struggles or his deliberate move we were both on the floor. It was during this controlled fall that I saw the knife, a large black-handled jackknife with a straight, tapering, blackened blade. My left side was pressed against the linoleum floor. He was on top, still behind me, still gripping fiercely. For the first time, he spoke.

"Don't scream," he said in a low monotone. "If you scream I'll cut your throat I swear to god I will."

"OK," I breathed. "OK." I noticed a sharp pain and stickiness in my left hand and realized I was pulling at his knife and cutting myself. But I couldn't keep my hands away. The pressure of the blade was so firm that, for the moment, it was my only focus, my only perceived danger.

He pulled me up with him and pushed me toward the corner utility-room door. It was at this point that my brain began to engage and that time slowed down. "Open the door," he said.

"I can't," I replied. (How could I even speak?) "It's locked."

"Open the door." Almost a growl in his voice this time.

"I can't I can't," I said, talking fast. "This door is always locked." But the tightening clamp of his arms and the deepening, slicing pressure of his knife forced my right hand to the doorknob. I thought of Paul, grateful that I had made love to him two days earlier. I thought: This is really happening. "I have money," I said, close to a whimper, knowing as I spoke that they were useless words. I turned the knob and opened the door.

Immediately he pushed me ahead of him into the utility

room, closing the door (presumably with his foot) behind us. With the sound of that closing door several things happened inside me simultaneously. I remembered, all in a single piece, a rape-prevention video seen while teaching high school twelve years ago. I remembered how I had broken up a fight between two boys in my classroom. I remembered a friend's escape from a rapist in Jamaica, when she distracted him with greed for her gold ring. Two messages sprang up: Stay calm. And: Use your wits; be clever. I forced myself to breathe more slowly. I forced my body to sag a bit against his.

The room was narrow, wrapping itself in an L around the back sides of the dryers I had been using so casually for the past five months. "Put your hands down," he ordered, pushing me toward the corner. "Put your hands down."

My hands fluttered at his arm, no longer pulling at it. "It's hard," I said.

"Put your hands down." Again, a hint of a growl. My hands dropped slowly to my thighs. I exhaled slowly.

"I noticed you out there," I said, groping for a beginning, knowing I had to start communicating in as normal way as possible. My hands jerked up.

"I know," he replied, walking me around the corner. "*Get your hands down.*" The knife blade jerked, breaking skin. Sharp. I forced my hands down. I forced my shoulders to sag.

In front of me the narrow room ended. Discarded clothes were scattered along the edges of the floor. A stack of white metal chairs faced us about halfway to the end wall. There they are, I thought, all this time. To my left three windows, each open about a foot, revealed the houses and parked cars on the street. My heart flew out to freedom between the square vertical bars and returned.

"Take your pants off," he said. With both hands I unbuttoned my Levi's, pushing them and my underpants down past my hips, squirming slightly. "Take your pants off."

"They're off they're off," I said. My voice had a breathy quality I didn't trust. But my breathing had slowed and I thought I could see how this would end. I could survive this.

"Take your shoes off. Come *on*."

"My shoes are tied with double knots," I said, twisting to the right in order to reach the laces. "Just let me bend over a little." His grip did not lessen; his knife remained at my throat. I clawed the laces loose, stalling for time. I pried each shoe off with my foot. Pushed from behind, I stepped out of my pants.

But for my crumpled socks I was naked now from the waist down, and felt a rush of coolness on my belly and thighs. From behind I could feel his flat stomach, his jeans, I think even his belt. I did not feel an erection. Most of all, I felt his gripping left arm. And the knife. I could hear his breathing in my right ear.

"I want you to masturbate," he said. His voice had softened, lowered. I reached with my right hand between my legs and began rubbing myself. I could feel the string of my tampon but decided to say nothing.

"This is fine for me," I said. "But what do you want me to do for you?" I heard a familiar tone in my own voice that heartened me.

"I want you to come," he answered.

"That's going to be hard." The explanation tumbled out. "In order to do that I need to relax, and I can't relax with the knife at my neck. What can I do for *you*?"

I continued masturbating, breathing slowly and deeply, hoping my response would defuse him. He pushed me farther into the room. Through two windows now I could see the safe world beyond. How I wanted to be out there.

With his left hand gripping my right shoulder, he turned me around to face him. The point of the knife pricked into my neck, just below my left ear. I looked into his face.

His hair looked even blonder in the light coming from his left, with reddish highlights. His skin was clear and fair, his cheekbones and jaw close shaven. A short nose. Tight lips. His eyes were unfocused, almost dusty, like the eyes of a cat. They terrified me. My face turned up to his, inhaling his breath, his cigarette smell and another undefined smell, I closed my eyes. "I don't want to see your face," I said. My right hand was still between my legs.

"You'll be all right," he said, and stepping me back farther, he pressed me down onto the stack of chairs.

"I don't know how to tell you this," I said, seated now on the top chair, my eyes still closed. "I'm menstruating and I have a tampon up there."

"Take it out."

"OK. But you might not want to look at this. It's pretty gross." My voice had lost its tension. I found the string and pulled out the tampon, considered for an instant throwing it out the window, dropped it instead on the floor. My left hand rested on the cool smooth arm of the chair; it throbbed from the cuts. He moved closer.

Probing gently, he put two or three fingers of his right hand into me. Then, in one swift gesture, he pulled all my shirts up so that they covered my face. I opened my eyes into bright turquoise light filtering through my sweatshirt. My arms were held by my shirts above my head. I flinched in the cool air, and at the thought of the knife. I felt utterly exposed and vulnerable. I thought, this is it.

He pressed me against the back of the chair. I was surprised next to feel his lips on my breasts. I couldn't bring myself to speak as he kissed first my left nipple and then my right. He ran his smooth right hand gently down the length of my torso. "You have a beautiful body," he said. His voice was breathless, softened. I thought: Should I say thank you?

In an instant, both his hands clenched around my throat. I was on the floor, on my back, and he on top of me, tightening his grip. Immediately my hands grabbed at his, clawing desperately. My mind screamed: Oh no I got one of these guys, *oh no!*

My breath rasped and labored as his thumbs pressed deeper, each painful gasp desperate, animal-sounding. This is what it is like to die in terror, I realized. This is what other women have felt. Paul's face, and a white sand beach with palm trees, and a blue sky, flashed through my brain.

My body was weakening rapidly, each breath noisier, more gurgly and more difficult to take. I felt myself poised just above my head, poised to leap out the window, to get out of here. *I don't want to die!* I screamed inwardly, my fingers digging into his. Then I remembered: Exhale to relax and conserve energy. Hoping to gain strength and time, I willed myself to exhale and go limp.

At that exact instant his hands unclenched. "You're a very lucky woman," he said hoarsely into my left ear. Gratefully, greedily, I breathed and swallowed. I felt him get off me, heard him step away. I didn't move.

"Are you going to run out of here?" I asked. My voice trembled.

His did not. "No. I'm going to walk out of here. And you're going to stay."

"How long do you want me to stay here?"

"Ten minutes," he said. I heard a rustle of clothing, sensed his presence now around the corner. "If you don't wait here ten minutes I'll come back and kill you."

I heard the doorknob turn, the door close. Then I heard the outside door slam shut. I counted to five and sat up, pulling my shirts down, trembling with relief and horror. I walked to my crumpled jeans, momentarily distracted by the absence of my underpants. As quickly as I could I pulled on my jeans, buttoning only the top button. Should I bother with my shoes? I quickly jammed them on.

"OK, Migael," I said. "You've got to stop him." I paused at the door and opened it slowly.

The laundromat was empty, silent, sunlit. My wet laundry lay in the dryers and in the wheeled basket, untouched. My jacket was on the table. My purse was gone. It was a startling still life.

I leaped from the door, scooped up my jacket, and ran out of the laundromat into the open protection of the boat shop across the street. I held up my bleeding left hand. I felt the sting of cuts on my neck.

6

READING THE CHARTS

This shaking keeps me steady, I should know.
What falls away is always. And is near.
I wake to sleep, and take my wakings slow.
I learn by going where I have to go.

—THEODORE ROETHKE

FRIDAY, APRIL 15

Three dreams last night. In the first, Paul and I were attempting to lower his sister from a balcony. Chris was balanced on a triangle, atop a pole. I then boarded a crowded bus, standing at the front near the door. Two young men, dressed in long black coats, black berets, with black curly hair walked toward me with guns. One tapped the muzzle of his machine gun on the floor around me. The other put the muzzle of his, as big around as a beer can, to my ear. Somehow I knew the guns weren't loaded, that they only wanted to scare me and everyone else.

I awoke. It was 4:00 A.M. An hour later I drifted into sleep again. This time I was in the Kwik-Kleen, alone, doing all my laundry in one washer and one dryer. I was using a dryer in the corner, where the utility doors are. It didn't seem to be working; all the clothes were tumbled in a tangled, damp mess. I dumped them all into a wheeled wire basket, bent to push it away. At the touch of the rubberized metal edge I started awake, shocked at the feel of it.

Paul went jogging early this morning, showered, left for work. After locking the hatch behind him I returned to bed, needing more sleep. In my dream I was adorning myself with pink flowers and netting. Looking in a mirror, I saw a wild-eyed woman crazily attired. I pulled everything from my head, horrified. I reeled to the bed, agonized by the sight of myself. I awoke, dry eyed. Twenty minutes had passed.

MONDAY, APRIL 18

Last night I dove back into sleep almost effortlessly the two times I awoke. The day was sunny. My session with Connie Tipton, over coffee at Julia's Café, eased rather than heightened any tension I had. Only when I described how I had apparently deflected death did my anxiety surface. Of course.

She looks as reassuring as she sounds in our phone conversations. Four years older than I am, just five feet tall (yet seated across from her I felt much smaller), hair about my color and length permed into fullness. She clearly takes her volunteer work for Seattle Rape Relief seriously, yet is ready to smile and patiently listen to the same thing over and over again.

"I really appreciate your calling twice a week," I said. "Knowing the phone's going to ring is all that gets me out of bed sometimes."

"I'm glad it's working," Connie said. "Let me know if it ever gets to be too often, or if you want to change the days."

"Do you work with all your clients like this?" I asked.

"It's different for everyone. I like meeting you this way. Nice to have a face to visualize when I'm talking on the phone. But many women prefer not to do this. It's entirely up to them. And some of them I only talk to once or twice anyway."

"Who decides that?"

"The client. Rape Relief believes that survivors should be given all the choices. They make the decisions, not us. That's why we wouldn't have called you, even if someone, say a friend, gave us your name. We do get requests like that, and our answer is always the same: It's up to the survivor, entirely. She's in control of her own healing."

Control. It had been taken from me so violently. Now it is gently being given back. By Connie when she waits for me to bring the session to an end, as though she has all the time in the world for me. By Paul when he lingers beside me in bed on the weekends, waiting until my need to hug or talk or cry subsides. By everyone who knows what I am only beginning to understand.

I launched the dinghy this afternoon and rigged her for a sail after first rowing a bit—I can feel the tenderness in my palms. Out in the blue of the ship canal I was relaxed, absorbed, happy. Along the docks, in boats, on barges and piers I saw only men. Most nodded or waved. It struck me that I live in a world that is predominantly male and have generally felt comfortable in it. Today, from my little sailboat, I felt some of that comfort. The sun, warmth, and pleasure of sailing made me feel a bit like myself again.

The sense of well-being persisted through my walk into downtown Ballard for hamburger buns and a newspaper, though I felt more vulnerable on foot and soon my wariness returned. I am beginning to believe that I will probably never see my attacker at large; if I do see him it will not be as a result of looking for him. In any case, I will never forget what he looks like. I have begun to let down my guard.

There is a new sliver of moon tonight. All the lights across the canal are reflected deep in the water, giving the far shore the appearance of a canyon wall. Everything is calm.

SATURDAY, APRIL 23

What began as such an up week has left me exhausted and perplexed. When the panic rose on schedule at 9:30 Tuesday morning, I reacted by sailing the dinghy in too much wind; my scramble to prevent capsizing temporarily distracted me. Never did accomplish anything that day. Perhaps I'd be better off accepting Tuesdays for what they are: hard.

The pace of Paul's work is quickening, as it was bound to, and he is faced with a new challenge: an Alaska project this summer. It was expected; almost every year he is given a complex architectural project that requires extra hours of work and an extended site visit, this time to Juneau, for review. Paul is energized by the demands of the job and by the prospect of being in Juneau. I, on the other hand, am anxious about my inability to support him as I have in the past. Not just with "atta-boys" and "you-can-do-its," but with keeping myself happy and occupied while he works overtime on specifications and presentation drawings. I have trouble now, when only his routine work separates us. I fear the withdrawal of his support that must occur if he is to prepare well.

I have felt this withdrawal only once before, when Paul returned from his business trip to Kodiak. He returned so full of his life away from me, full of the news of healthy, happy people I know only from a distance, that I could find no place for myself. I was at once isolated, left behind, testy. His irritation with me caused me to withdraw, which irritated him further. How will we cope with the known stresses of a major architecture project? Our old give-and-take is now so lop-sided, put off balance by my need to avoid any kind of conflict, even a healthy one.

"I've been talking with Connie about this," I said last week over dinner. "She says that if I know something hard is coming up, it might help if I try to make everything else easier."

Paul nodded and suggested we wipe the May calendar free of

everything that would complicate his increased work schedule and our time together. "Would that help?" he asked.

"Yeah," I said, relieved. "I know you miss all the social life we used to have, but that would help a lot."

"I do miss it," he agreed. "But it's like the guy from Rape Relief said the other day—you know, the guy Connie recommended—it's all about control. When too many things are going on, it can make you feel like everything's out of control. You don't need *that*."

Later in the evening, we came up with the idea of my traveling to Juneau ahead of him to visit my sister and our friends, but mostly to give Paul some freedom during the final days of his project. The thought of leaving Paul for so many days still scares me, but Connie's counseling helps. "Anxious as you are," Connie said on the phone, "I hear strength in your voice. You're taking hold of the problem, getting yourself prepared."

My mother called yesterday morning to tell me she was thinking of me, to tell me she loves me, and to apologize for my father's response. "He really cares about you," she said. "It's always been hard for him to say anything about his feelings, but he really does care. You know that." Yes, I wanted to tell her. I know. We all know. But I can't help him with it now.

Both my father's calls last week unsettled me. The first was to tell me he and my brother were "having problems" over me. (I was afraid to ask what that meant, and he never explained.) Of course, my father was trying to say he was concerned about me, but his words made me feel as though I have handled everything wrong, as though I were being chided for the way I reacted to my brother's visit. I felt almost responsible for the attack itself. My father's second call was to talk about books. The subject (historical fiction) was harmless, but I couldn't touch it. All I could think of was how critical he has been of my "knee-jerk liberal" recommendations in the past. I kept my thoughts to myself.

My sleep these past two nights has deteriorated once more, last night's especially. I think I had a touch of stomach flu and know I was feeling sad and hurt. I was in bed at 8:30, asleep after Paul joined me by 10:00. Alternately chilled and hot, my stomach cramping and all my muscles aching, I awoke at 1:30. For most of the remaining night I lay in the grip of memory and illness, drifting in and out of dreams. In my final dream my brother Charles and my parents had moved aboard *Orca*. I was attempting to get dressed. I wanted to wear my new black dress, but it had a gaping hole below the neckline. When I darned it up, another appeared, as though the dress were decaying in my hands. I went below to find something else to wear. All the lockers had been rearranged; the pans had been removed from beneath the stove and canned goods put in their place. Charles had moved his clothes into my lockers. The lower drawer was full of men's underwear either too big or too small for me. Charles mumbled pompously when I objected. I ended up screaming, crying, throwing everything everywhere. Enraged and wailing, I threw myself onto the starboard couch. I awoke, trembling. Paul gathered me into his arms.

Portland, Oregon
April 24, 1988

Dearest Migael,

It was good to hear your voice; you sound strong and in control, but your honest appraisal of your emotional state distresses me. Oh, of course, I say to myself, why *wouldn't* she be going through all the usual heavy load of stuff? Still, it causes me much anguish to think of you in pain and fear. For you, my dear, are one of my own personal examples of strength. You seem full of so many qualities I would like to emulate—courage and joy tops among them. It infuriates me—absolutely enrages me—that some asshole could have the power to dim these qualities in you. Grr . . . I shake my fist at the world! This seems to be my angry stage of life, and now I have one more thing to be mad about. Anyway, I think of you with tender concern every single day— many times. You and Paul are in my thoughts. Just know that.

I am simply loving the challenge and structure of my studies these days. I am very far away from actually receiving a graduate degree, but the mere fact that I get up and walk to campus, that I sit in class and take notes, that I laugh and talk with my co-students at coffee afterward, amazes me. How quickly this new life of mine has taken shape. I wish you could share with me the heady atmosphere I now occupy.

Care and comfort,
Anna

TUESDAY, APRIL 26

Unbelievably, yesterday was the first time I had been alone with my mother since my assault. Her invitation to take me to lunch had been timid and hopeful; I accepted instantly.

"Wouldn't you like something more than a salad?" she said after we'd ordered. "Maybe a sandwich? Or some soup?"

"I'm not real hungry," I answered, shrugging off her questions. I could see her weighing me with her eyes.

She bit her lip and looked away. "I finally called Seattle Rape Relief last week," she said after a long pause. "The woman I talked to was so kind. I felt much better afterward. I wish I had called them two months ago."

I was nodding, sipping my coffee, hoping she would keep talking. Her voice was suddenly as soothing as a lullaby.

"I want you to know that it's all right if you can't see us— your father and me—right now. I think I understand. I remember how hard it was when Mother died. I . . . I missed her so much, and sometimes I'd walk by her room and just start crying, and your father would seem almost . . . impatient."

She smiled slightly, but her eyes darkened with grief. I remembered how I had held her as my grandmother's draped form was wheeled down the hall of the nursing home. How small my mother had seemed then.

"Anyway," she continued, "your father will be fine. Don't worry about him through all this. I can take care of him. You need to take care of yourself."

"That's what my counselor says." The tightness below my ribs released. "She says that a crisis doesn't always bring people closer. Sometimes it magnifies a problem you thought you'd resolved long ago but didn't, not really. She says it's best to put the problem aside and work on the more immediate ones. I *do* need to stay away from him right now." This was incredible. My mother had just given me what I would never have had the strength to ask for. "But . . . we can talk from time to time—can't we? Without him?"

"Oh, my dear," she said, searching through the salad set before her as though there were a treasure hidden in the lettuce. "We sure can." When she looked up her face was radiant. Both of us, simultaneously, began to eat.

THURSDAY, APRIL 28

In the last few weeks I have been impatient with the time it takes to clean all our clothes in the one washer and dryer at Stan and Teri's. Using a laundromat is so much faster; I can do a week's worth of wash in an hour and a half. When I asked Connie and Stan and Teri for their professional advice on going to a laundromat, they all responded pretty much the same: "Go ahead and give it a try. If it doesn't feel right, walk out."

So yesterday I packed up the laundry and drove to Wallingford, to the staff-attended laundromat I used five years ago, before we sailed to Alaska. Every sound, smell, and gesture was sharply significant: inserting quarters into slots, pushing in the upright silver rounds with the palm of my right hand until the motor engaged and the sound of rushing water was heard. I fingered the rubberized edge of the wheeled metal basket and noted the angle of my body as I bent to push it. I was alert, but not alarmed, by the smell and feel of damp laundry as I filled three dryers. Loading quarters and flipping knobs I thought: At last, I have completed what was disrupted three months ago.

I was not alone. A young Asian woman with long dark hair was folding clothes and fussing with the dry cleaning. She was also talking with the repairman, who used to be the owner. We recognized each other and filled in the intervening years. A young man with a blond brush cut walked in and out with a single load of laundry; from the questions he asked it was his first time there. I was aware of him at all times. A young woman with a little boy entered, talking excitedly about a friend now pregnant with her second set of twins.

It is certainly a busier place than the Kwik-Kleen, more cramped, with fewer machines. I can understand why, up until February 9, I liked the other so much: light, spacious, comfortable seating, quiet. And I can see why my attacker found it so appealing as well: enough room to act, minimal pedestrian traffic, deserted midmorning but for one small woman with a predictable routine. Well, I shall prefer for now the busyness, the awkward chairs, the cluttered tables. The sun still shines through the corner windows, and the place opens up early enough. Well worth the extra five-minute drive.

When I returned home I glanced over at *Eagle*, moored on the other dock, and thought of Ed. It has become a habit of mine. Since the day I'd broken the news to him—I was in deep shock then, I now realize, my neck still bruised and cut—I had come to regard him as a source of comfort. Not just because he is a former cop who long ago accepted violence as a reality but also because his steady presence as a friend who lives aboard nearby helps me feel less isolated, more protected. Yesterday's need for a roasting pan gave me an excuse to walk to his boat on the other dock and interrupt his fo'c'sle work. He seemed to welcome the break. Our light small talk at the galley table turned into a cup of coffee, then to talk of his hopes to write during his forthcoming cruise to Hawaii.

"Like my journal," I offered, "which I've been keeping since my assault."

Instead of letting it pass, Ed set down his cup and reached for his cigarettes. "How are you doing since your attack?" he asked.

"It's very hard," I said. Knowing he cared, I opened up and answered. And learned.

I had hoped to hear from him something firsthand about living through a near-death experience. I assumed his years with the police department would have given him at least one. Not so. He had never been at another's "mercy," he felt, as I had been. But he had observed that those who had, the "Vietnamers" on his SWAT team, reacted to danger differently than the others, were more effective and alert. He had been impressed with the seasoning their Vietnam experience seemed to have given them.

I sighed over the awakening of this alertness in me, the compulsion to note everyone and everything around me. Ed merely shrugged. "You know," he said, "alertness was my life's work."

"Do you still look at everybody?" I asked.

"I look at *everybody*," he said. "You get used to it. It fits the way the world really is."

"Like the alertness when cruising," I added. Of course. Always attending to the sound of the engine, the surface of the water, the look of the sky, the instruments and charts has become second nature to me but has not interfered with the pleasure of cruising. If anything, the pleasure is more intense.

The insight that Ed so casually handed me across the table, that he had long taken for granted, delighted me. Why not welcome this sharper focus? I felt like I had just picked up a small essential tool, so well handled and familiar to others that its value was now unnoticed.

So I am always at sea. Perhaps this is why I immediately

relaxed on our cruise to the San Juan Islands last March. Then the charged awareness was familiar. Years of cruising have taught me to always read the charts, to anticipate and prepare for the worst. What happened to me in that laundromat is bound to transfer these lessons to my larger, more complicated shore life. The shoals and rocks I once overlooked because they never harmed me or anyone I loved now seem so obvious. Not every rock is charted, but now I have the eyes and wits to look for those that are.

7

REVERSALS

*There is only the fight to recover what has been lost and found
and lost again and again . . .*

—T. S. Eliot

MONDAY, MAY 2

What is happening to me? Since Thursday night I have been increasingly remote and withdrawn. The lives around me are full and preoccupied. I am surrounded by an isolating membrane that only the strongest, most demonstrative love can penetrate. I want to cling, but sense that my fierceness will repel.

It has been three months now—one quarter of a year overlaid by fear, sorrow, pain, confusion, exhaustion, and terrifying memory. They darken even the brightest days. Where is the sharp joy of being alive? What am I doing with my "second chance" at life? With all the strength I can muster I am accomplishing so little.

It was a bad idea to entertain last week, two nights in a row, with friends who are unable to comfort me or even acknowledge my wounds. There I was, in the impossible position of reassuring others, pretending that everything is fine. Exhausted by the effort, I could only retreat into a corner of the couch and wait out the evening. It saddens me to realize that there are some friends I need to avoid for a while. Paul is right; it's best to keep our social life quiet.

A good walk this morning around Green Lake, with a woman I worked for almost five years ago. Gently, she opened the subject of a writing job this summer. The prospect baffles me. She thinks I am strong, but I don't feel capable yet of all the concentration and organization that writing a technical manual demands. Flattered, though unsure, I said I was interested. But I should have been more honest with her. Instead, I hid my feelings in our public walk, talk, and breakfast. I buried them in the newsprint of the paper we read over coffee. I zipped them up into my jacket, half knowing they would emerge when I was alone, defenseless.

Washington, D.C.
May 3, 1988

Dear Migael,

Thank you so much for your letter. I imagine that you are faced these days with many people who do not know what to say. Glad that my book has been a word of encouragement of any kind, but also feeling inadequate in the face of what was done to you. I am moved and angry at once. How brave you are to write.

Much of your life must seem utterly different now, and much of it incongruously the same. I do believe, however, from my experience of you and from your letter, that you are a person who is for life and that your spirit will triumph. All love and prayers for your ongoing strength. I study your courage.

A former and present student,
Laura

THURSDAY, MAY 5

I was jumpy while my clothes were washing and drying at the Wallingford laundromat yesterday. I sat, read, and observed. I felt a little nauseated, as though waiting for something to happen. Was this what *he* felt, I wonder, as he waited and watched for my most vulnerable moment?

Relieved to be done, I carried my basket of clean laundry out the door only to discover that my car was impounded. Jesus, I thought, when am I going to get this laundry business right? Margaret laughed and shook her head when she arrived to rescue me. "Well," she said, "I guess we should consider this an improvement."

An item in an old copy of the *North Seattle Press* has re-charged my wariness. It described the attack on a woman alone in her Ballard home south of Market Street, the attack Detective Peters had told me about last March. Through the short, almost flip description I saw the subtle signs of the attacker: patient, desperate, on the edge of carelessness. He must be driving the police crazy.

So I am back to searching as well as scanning every face, to feeling responsible as a witness against a man who is devastating lives and is, as far as I'm concerned, capable of killing. In the Safeway last night my heart contracted as a man walked up the aisle behind me. Fear has settled back in.

Just one dream two nights ago. I was caring for a frail sandy-haired baby who hung suspended by his neck in a doorway. He was alive, screaming, his neck slashed in one clean cut. The wound wasn't deep, but it gaped red in his struggles. I did my best to soothe him, but I did not lift him from his noose.

MONDAY, MAY 9

A flat emptiness has settled over me this evening. This no longer surprises me after a couple of full, productive days.

What used to give me so much satisfaction now does so only temporarily. Today's painting and sanding on *Orca* was smooth and speedy, but as soon as I finished I ceased to think about it. I feel the first stirrings of "Why bother?" Yet tomorrow I hope to push through this alarming fatalism and continue, bringing the aft-cabin remodel a little closer to completion.

The complexity of *Orca* building and maintenance overwhelms me to a degree I would never have believed. Three months ago the prospect of tearing apart an entire cabin and reshaping it invigorated me. I was prepared to tackle it simultaneously with a new teaching job, was in fact preparing for both in January as I filled out application forms and hauled junk out to the shop. Now I depend so heavily on Paul's lead. He, who is accustomed to doing a dozen projects at once, is proceeding more methodically to accommodate me. I am doing well enough with a day like today, busy and entirely alone. I feel I am exactly where I belong. But I miss the enthusiasm and initiative I once took for granted. These ignited yesterday when we worked out some locker arrangements, and Saturday when I sanded the oak hatches, but they are easily extinguished.

What extinguishes them are the flashbacks. Saturday afternoon I was stopped in my tracks by the clear memory of sound: my own labored, rasping breath, sliding into a choked gurgle as he strangled me. My actual surroundings dissolved as the fear surfaced. Paul's hugs and words returned me to the present—a good hour later. Today a recurring memory tapped me on the shoulder every time my mind drifted as I painted: Two arms grip me unexpectedly from behind, pressing a knife to my throat. I pushed this aside only by returning to wariness.

TUESDAY, MAY 17

My spirit appears to be settling down, calming. I have had one good week and appear to be having another. Generally I sleep six hours every night, only occasionally interrupted. Sometimes I awake with easy thoughts. And I have caught myself singing and humming to myself—a very encouraging sign.

Paul's aft-cabin work is fueling my own, keeping me busy, distracted, satisfied. He is doing a terrific job back there. *Orca* is providing amazing therapy for us both as we learn to compromise lovingly, as we laugh over harebrained ideas, as we interlock our work without interfering with each other. How fitting that it is our final big project aboard, and our bedroom.

Still, my mind is never far from my attack or my attacker. Every new place or person is a question mark: Does he shop here? drink here? live here? And my time alone off *Orca* has an edge of tension: What will I do if he turns the corner up there? If he walks in the shop while I'm painting the cabinets, how should I act? I no longer seem to relive the assault in those dark hours when I cannot sleep, but I am filled with recriminations: I should have kept my eyes wide open and picked up more clues; I should have regained my wits more quickly and talked more persuasively; I should have looked down the street so I could have spotted his unhurried retreat. Foolish wheel spinning.

Tired of speculation, I called Detective Peters this morning for a reality check. Nothing new, but two subsequent attacks in the evening on the street—random actions that may point to the same man. Careless enough to give the police some hope. This news was pretty much what I expected; I am amazed that any of these cases get solved at all.

SUNDAY, MAY 22

All week Paul had been planning for my forty-first birthday. We had celebrated Margaret's at the top of the Space Needle last fall and Jack's at the top of the Seafirst Building only two weeks ago. Our spirits high, we looked forward to celebrating mine at the top of the Stouffer Madison Hotel.

It began so beautifully. Paul arrived home about five, bearing birthday mail and three red roses. Debra called from

Juneau, excited about my visit next month. She described the cruise ships in the harbor, the mountains and eagles, the fish we would catch together. Listening to her was like opening a present. Then Paul and I walked into downtown Ballard for a newspaper, stopping for a beer on the way back. The evening was warm, sunny, full of lengthening shadows and promise.

The first stirrings of dissatisfaction occurred when I tried to pin one of the rosebuds onto my lapel. I winced when the stem broke. At Margaret's, I sent Paul back to *Orca* for a change of shoes.

In the car I became impatient with Paul. He, too, seemed impatient, with the pace, with Jack's route to the restaurant. I was beginning to have misgivings about the place. What if I hadn't chosen the best one? Would we arrive too late?

The restaurant was filled with gowned and tuxedoed high school kids; it was a prom night. I tried to feel their youthful excitement. Paul and Jack horsed around as we ordered. The waiter was invited to tell a joke; emboldened by his first he launched into two others whose racism was so offensive that Paul (thankfully) spoke up. Awkwardness hung in the air.

And, for me, nausea. Halfway through my Caesar salad I stopped eating. I'd had a Scotch before the appetizer; perhaps that was the cause. How was I going to make it through the main course? And dessert! I forced myself to hold on. Luckily the prawns were delicious and the nausea subsided. But the wine was bitter in my mouth, and there was too much too-rich food remaining on my plate when I put my fork down.

Our shared desserts seemed a pointless formality. The waiter placed the lighted candle in front of Jack, not me. It took all the control I had not to burst into tears when Margaret asked me if I'd made a wish.

The three of them continued their quick talk and laughter. I slowly retreated, unable to capture their light spirits. I wondered: Where is the joy I want to feel? In the car as we drove away, I looked at Paul, fear in my eyes. I inhaled, hoping to hold on a bit longer. A roaring rose in my ears. Paul scooted to my side of the seat. With one hand covering my face I began to cry.

I couldn't stop. Not while standing on the crest of Queen Anne Hill, overlooking the city, not while trying to follow Paul and Margaret's attempts at distracting conversation, not while sitting, parked, near Jack and Margaret's house. Even sandwiched between the three of them I couldn't shake my grief for what I have lost, or my fear for what lies ahead. Paul parted our four embraces and drove me home. I cried myself to sleep in his arms.

Yesterday the struggle continued. I tried to ignore it as I sanded, painted, and oiled, as I cleaned the dinghy and rowed across the canal. But slowly, the very brightness of the day revealed what I have been hiding from everyone, even from myself.

In two days I see a specialist for a breast exam and biopsy. The briefest flicker of worry passed over my doctor's face when he felt the lump over a week ago and recommended this next procedure. And how did I respond? With complete denial, refusing to accept anything but the best result. All week I have said to myself, Oh that. It's nothing. Forget it. I have made light of it even with Paul and have told no one else.

Last night Paul and I checked out a video from the store next to the Kwik-Kleen. What an innocent-looking, bright place that laundromat is. The barred windows in back are still sinister; I know what that narrow, L-shaped room looks like. I was surprised at how easily I could see into it, though I didn't look hard. I was a little afraid that I would see myself—gripped from behind, groping for the right words and actions—looking back at me.

WEDNESDAY, MAY 25

Just returned from yoga and feel settled at last. I won't know the results of the biopsy until Friday, but my anxieties, at least, have been eased.

Thank god I opened up. I struggled against it Monday morning, but couldn't disguise my distress when Paul called from the office or, especially, when Connie called from Rape Relief, as she does every Monday.

"So how did the weekend go?" she asked.

My voice broke. "I don't know what to do."

"Take all the time you need," Connie said, instantly calming, patient. I stumbled through the whole story. Why had it taken me so long to do this? "Of course you feel horrible," she said. "On top of everything you are going through, of course."

Gradually, I gained control of my tears and my voice. Gently, she revealed that she has gone through the same experience, that her lump was benign as mine is likely to be, but that the thought of breast cancer terrifies her, and of course I'm worried. She offered to come over; the sight of her on the dock twenty minutes later was unbelievably comforting. And she was ready to make plans.

"OK," she said, after drawing out my fear over a cup of tea at the galley table. "All we have to do, can do at this time, is get through the exam. You don't have to think beyond it yet. How will you get to Group Health? I'd be glad to give you a ride and stay with you. What about Paul? Will he want to be there?" We sifted through the details, arranged for her to drive me, Paul to take me home afterward. By the time she left I was shored up with hope and purpose.

But over dinner the fear returned. For the first time Paul and I talked about what lies ahead if the biopsy results show cancer. We held each other and cried. We walked for a newspaper in the long twilight. That night I slept deeply, a full eight hours, as I have not been able to do in months.

The nurses and the physician at the specialty clinic treated the biopsy as simple routine. That helped. But the needle used to draw tissue from the lump was long, seemed to pierce into the very center of me. After the remarkably brief procedure I was calm and eager to get on with the day, which was sunny and warm. Paul went back to work. Needing a break, I wandered over to Ed's boat. His galley table and floor were covered with charts, the charts covered with notes he and his wife had made on their cruise to Hawaii, Australia, and Alaska two years ago. Perfect! We unrolled his Alaska charts, talked about passages and anchorages we knew, future adventures.

Back aboard *Orca,* I was psyching myself up for a walk when Margaret arrived, unannounced. "Paul just called me," she said, smiling and shaking her head. Her embrace was full of understanding and love.

I tried to explain why I had not told her about the lump in my breast, how I didn't want to give her another one of my burdens, how unfair it would have seemed to do so. After all, it could be nothing. She gently dismissed my excuses. "If you can take it," she said, "so can the rest of us."

We sat in the almost blinding sunlight on the aft deck, watched the boats and barges of the ship canal, absorbed the busyness of the water and wind. We talked of all we had been through together since February, how different the world seemed now.

"I've never heard the whole story of the attack," Margaret said, hesitation in her voice. "I talked with a woman at Rape Relief, and she suggested it could help us both. If you were willing."

"Yes," I agreed. "It does help. It's a hard story to hear, and a hard one to tell, but it helps."

"I'm ready now," Margaret said, "if you are. I have time to hear it all. And," she added, "time to recover, later."

I settled myself cross-legged against the cockpit bench. I looked around at the bright blueness everywhere. I closed my eyes and hefted my laundry basket into the laundromat. The man sitting in the corner looked up.

FRIDAY, MAY 27

Waiting out a rainy afternoon. Paul should be home soon. Sometime in the next hour one burden will be either lifted from me entirely or increased horribly. And yet much as I know the biopsy results are pivotal today, I can barely concentrate on them.

Yesterday I saw him. As I was driving north to shop at Safeway I spotted him walking out of a convenience store on the corner, sipping on a straw from a large red soft-drink cup. The first thing I noticed was his hair, how it parted and shone in the sun, straight, full, and sandy brown. All the pieces fell together as I had hoped they would: the shape of his head, the set of his shoulders as he walked, the angle of his neck as he bent down to sip, the color of his skin and his height. I noted his navy-blue jacket and straight-legged baggy white pants, which somehow looked like uniform pants. And the jarring item that didn't fit my memory, his black-rimmed glasses.

He walked with the light across Market Street, in the exact opposite direction I was traveling. Though I couldn't have observed him for more than a few seconds, I was so struck by his appearance that I immediately made a right turn in order to circle back for another look, to catch him as he would walk east when the light turned.

Then it all fell apart. Two busses stopped between us, or he had walked faster than I thought, or he had vanished. Perhaps he had hopped on one of the busses. In any case, he was gone. The press of traffic pushed me around the corner back in the direction of Safeway. I thought: Was it really him? Am I sure enough to call this one in? Those black glasses confused me, undermined my confidence.

Thoroughly distracted, trying desperately to forget that fleeting image, I parked in front of Safeway, walked into the store, grabbed a shopping cart. Automatically I picked up bread, some fruit. All the alarms in my body were ringing loudly, trying to override my denial. The desire to escape immobilized me. Standing in the produce section, a cabbage somehow in my hand, my ears roared, my gaze became fixed and glazed. Get to a phone, I said to myself. Do it *now.*

Even after I walked to the north end of the store, zombielike, and stood at the pay phone, I hesitated. What if it wasn't him?

Two teenagers at the phone next to me disturbed my concentration and resolve. I exhaled deeply, misdialed 911, dialed again. I blurted my news into the receiver. Patiently, the 911 operator on the other end asked for details. The names of streets jumbled in my mouth. And I was stopped dead by his final question: "Do you want a patrol car sent?" Unable to make a decision, not understanding his reason for asking (I was, after all, safe), I stammered and finally said, "No."

Back in the grocery store I retrieved my cart and mechanically finished my shopping. Something wasn't right, I knew, so before I drove home I went back to the pay phone and called Detective O'Brien, who was in, thank god, and whose response was immediate and focused. He would call me at home later.

So there I was again, wheeling my cart out to *Orca,* hauling bags from the same store, all my world in upheaval. Yet I clung to routine as before, putting away groceries (I had made some bizarre purchases), intent on picking up Paul at five. O'Brien called for additional details, general questions about my 911 call. I sensed that I hadn't made the urgency clear, that I may have blown it. Certainly I wasn't 100 percent positive of the identification, which is precisely why I'd driven around for another look. All the plans I'd made for such an event had collapsed because of my uncertainty. I asked O'Brien what I should have done.

"Try to keep him in view," he explained. "Follow discreetly if possible. If asked about sending a car . . ."

"Say yes," I finished for him, feeling foolish.

"Yes," he emphasized. I could hear the disappointment in his voice. A sense of my own failure took root. Even his reassurances that I was not wasting his time with my uncertainty, that I can call him with any question or observation, did not stop its disturbing growth.

That night I experienced all the disbelief, shock, fear, and relief in condensed form. At times I was buoyant and talkative. Then I would lapse into silence, cringing in a corner. Or tremble and cry. Paul, whose response was to play busily with the new microwave oven, observed that my mood changed about every twenty minutes.

O'Brien called at eleven that night, spoke with Paul. "Tell her not to lose heart," he said. "There was an attack two nights ago. It may give us a fingerprint." This morning I talked to O'Brien, learned a few more details. The latest victim described a "sweet," underlying smell, as I had. If not alcohol or cologne or marijuana, what was it? Most important, O'Brien reminded me to trust my instincts. He's right; instinct has stood by me so far. But the fear warps it.

SATURDAY, MAY 28

It was wonderful to be able to look at Paul last night, give him the news that the biopsy showed no cancer, and watch the tension drain from his face. In his embrace I felt it drain from his body. "You've pulled a heart out of the deck," he said. "At last." Through dinner we fixed on the airy happiness of the moment. Soon afterward he was napping on the couch. I realized then that, all along, Paul had done the heavy worrying for me.

A good sleep last night, though I am running down after hearing this morning's news from Brad. Helen has breast cancer, has had it since late April, has had the lump removed and starts radiation therapy next month. Could we find moorage for them in Seattle, so they can live aboard their boat when their teaching jobs end next month and avoid the almost daily commute from Port Townsend?

"Don't give it another thought," I said after pumping Brad for more information and talking with Helen. "There's plenty of moorage here at our marina. I'm sure something can be arranged. And we're going to want you close by." Jesus, I thought. Can I possibly help her?

8

OUTER POINT

The irony of man's condition is that the deepest need is to be free of the anxiety of death and annihilation; but it is life itself that awakens it, and so we must shrink from being fully alive.

—ERNEST BECKER
The Denial of Death

WEDNESDAY, JUNE 1

This morning it finally awoke: rage. As I was sanding drawer glides in the aft cabin, thinking about Helen, the image of my attacker sprang to mind. God *damn* you, I thought. You are the cause of all my pain. You have robbed me of so much energy and peace. You have crippled my ability to help my friends. See what you have done!

If I saw him now my impulse would be to attack. For an hour this morning I lay in bed fantasizing, not about how to catch him but how to entice and hurt him. It's about time I felt this emotion, so powerful it brings tears. Last week was such a hard lesson to me. I am broken so easily by the hardships of others, of myself. And why? Because one hateful, evil man collides with me, randomly selects me as the object of his violence. God *damn* him.

Trying very hard today to be productive. It is a real effort, even though progress in the aft cabin is important to me, something I know will give me a sense of accomplishment. Less than four months ago a list of projects and errands energized me every time. Couldn't wait to get at them. Now I react with such reserve, proceed with comparative listlessness.

This same mood persists in planning for my trip to Juneau next Friday. It is what I have decided to do. Leaving Paul alone to prepare presentation drawings for his Alaska project is the only support I can give him now. He deserves and needs time away from me.

We will be apart only five days and nights. I will be with friends who love me. My sister and her family live there. But I am still afraid. When I left Juneau one year ago I was strong, adventurous, happy. Now I fear the image of myself that Juneau will reflect back to me.

WEDNESDAY, JUNE 8

Thank god! Today is my third day of normal Migael-ness. It feels so good to have myself back. Each day has been busy and self-directed. I am making progress on the aft cabin and am looking forward to completing the next phase, a phase that I defined. My mind drifts to pleasant trivialities. I have even caught myself walking or driving without memories of the attack foremost on my consciousness. And though I still scan every face, I do so almost routinely; alertness doesn't seem so exhausting. (Perhaps this is the vigilance Ed spoke of; if so, I can live with it.) It has been almost two weeks since I felt this peace of mind, and now it seems stronger than my previous spell.

Talked with Detective Peters this morning, to let him know I'm leaving town. The Ballard assault cases continue to pile up—a diverse mess. The latest occurrence shows signs of the same man, though this time he managed to "perform" (Peters's word). Maybe he's finally figured it out? In any event, this call left me strangely unsettled. Perhaps it was Peters's use of the word "wrong" when he referred to actions by a victim that could lead to homicide. Or it could be the unspoken message that Peters's knowledge of my whereabouts isn't that critical. Certainly the case has moved well beyond me. Until the rapist is caught or I have useful information (I still wince at my reaction when I thought I spotted him two weeks ago), I am pretty much beside the point.

Last Sunday morning I put to rest an impulse that has been nudging me for months. With Paul I walked south from the Kwik-Kleen, on the route my attacker walked when he left me lying behind the dryers. I saw the trees, green and leafy now, the houses, the yards. Glanced into the garage where he had tossed my purse into a canoe that now lay tipped on its side. Children called to each other on the corner. Folks gardened in their yards. A dog wagged its tail from behind a fence. We walked past the scene of his second assault, near Gilman Park: A young boy and an old man mowed the lawn around the duplex. A baseball game was in session across the street. Normal, happy living. Though the spot of evil almost without a doubt lives within a mile of our walking (we may have passed his house), goodness thrives and grows. Goodness prevails.

FRIDAY, JUNE 10

It was Paul who gave me the strength to walk away from him and into this airplane. Every minute after he stepped aboard *Orca* from work was full. Our talk was of the future, our next phone contact, our next meeting. Our lovemaking was splendid, triumphant, intertwined as always with flashbacks of rape, climaxing as always with an intensity of safety, love, and life. So though I caught my breath as I walked down the ramp toward the plane, and hesitated before entering it, I was able to push ahead eagerly.

My physical presence on this plane astonishes me. The first strong associations are of smell and touch. The dry air, overlaid with the smell of kerosene, immediately recalls my emotional state four months ago when we flew to St. Martin. I am almost afraid to breathe; I do not want to slip back to that world where everything, even my body, was new and frightening. My pulse is racing. I drift into daydream and flashback.

What a plane ride that was, February eleventh and twelfth. I remember only scattered details: Paul guiding me on board, to my seat, never far from me, almost always touching me. It was he who kept track of our bags, our papers, and tickets. He made the decisions, gathered up pillows and blankets, urged me to eat and drink when I could. I remember sleeping fitfully on the first leg, sitting bolt upright. It was early morning, and dark, when we landed in Atlanta. The orange juice went to my head like wine. The light and voices, the business men and women, seemed like dream figures. It was in Atlanta that I entered a restroom alone; I braced myself before opening the door.

We are beginning our descent into Juneau. Soon we will penetrate the white fluff that spreads below in every direction. Fear, joy, and excitement rush up.

MONDAY, JUNE 13

The view from Debra's apartment is spectacular, an Alaska version of the one in St. Martin. Auke Bay is a frosted mirror, disturbed only by a single white trawler heading northwest. The mountains on Douglas Island and, to the north, toward Glacier Bay, are blue-green and snow topped, only partially obscured by clouds. The tide is low, leaving the beach mottled gold. Far to the west, a high pressure is building—an almost yellow streak of clear sky.

I am grateful that Alaska has covered and softened her beauty with clouds so far. I could not have stood up to her full brightness. My first sight as the plane descended was overwhelming enough. And the Mendenhall Glacier deepens and glows best in the gray.

All the first evening and next day I felt mildly drugged. I noted each leaf, the texture of cloud. I breathed the sweet alder. My rubber boots sank into the soil.

Though I knew and feared it would happen, I couldn't have predicted when I would break. The precipitating event was my sister's now year-old pain over her son's mental illness.

It's true I look and act like myself, deceptively so. I explain my altered ways, but unless these are observed they are easily dismissed. What is a throbbing wound looks to some like a smooth, healed-over scar. So it is only natural that Gloria would open up to me when we were fishing with Debra and voice her most fearsome thoughts. Her belief that death is not the worst thing, that Allen's mental illness is a more difficult struggle, struck me to the core. I ignored it; she repeated it more fiercely. The message in her face (*"Listen to me. I am in crisis"*) stopped me from voicing the memories that surfaced so strongly. Gloria was voicing her own anger and sorrow, but she had touched my *reality*.

I tried to tuck all this away, to be both a confider and a confidante; the struggle eventually broke me. Gradually I became nervous, agitated. At the grocery store with Debra to get salmon steaks (our fishing adventure left us skunked) I clenched and unclenched my hands on stiff arms, flinched when strangers approached or, especially, when they passed behind me. Simple decisions (which video? who to call?) baffled me. Sitting on the bed, my hand on the phone, I realized I was incapable of answering a simple "How are you?" My heart pounded and my ears roared. I walked into the kitchen where Debra was starting dinner, burst into tears, and asked for a hug. I fell—the long, weightless, agonized free fall—and Debra caught me.

WEDNESDAY, JUNE 15

For the first time, I forgot it was Tuesday.

Monday had been dazzling and full. I was infected with the Juneau sunny-day madness. Debra's treat for me, a helicopter trip to the Mendenhall Glacier, heightened every sense. What an unreal landscape! We walked on the ancient ice just long enough for the biting wind and its uncaring beauty to penetrate hands, face, and consciousness.

Even there I could not escape myself. Memory rode up with us, in the form of our pilot. His general appearance and especially his voice (a chillingly similar voice) were so distracting that I forgot my anxieties about flying in a helicopter for the first time.

Debra delivered me to Scott and Alice's little yellow house about 5:00 P.M., and a whole new day began. Slowly, I began to slip. Too many beginnings, too much news, were unfolding around me. I silently choked down the sadness and loneliness, using precious energy to keep up appearances. Why do I do this? Scott and Alice are as ready to comfort me now as they were when we cruised together last March.

I awoke already exhausted. I fumbled through morning routines, anxious to make decisions for myself, frustrated at my inability to do so. After several false starts I walked out the door and into the sun, on the familiar walk to Aurora Harbor.

I ran into myself everywhere. The old Migael emerged, taunted me with her energy and hopefulness. It was like walking with my own ghost. How buoyantly I once walked the path to the harbor. How my heart would leap to the future as I descended the steep ramp. How confidently I rounded each corner and smiled at each stranger. How strong I was then. I struggled against my sudden tears.

Walking the docks revived me. Comforted by the drone of high-speed sanders, I wandered among the familiar tugs and fishing boats, chatted with old neighbors, watched a friend rewire a power post at the head of the float where we used to live aboard *Orca*. Above us Mount Juneau rose straight up, the chill of the icefields beyond palpable even in the sun. With reluctance I left the harbor to meet Gloria across the street for coffee.

This time I felt stronger, able to really listen to her. I could allow myself to see my sister's struggles, even explain some of my own, without anguish. Though I was open and honest, I was aware that I was protecting her from myself. Possibly she was doing the same, though the decisiveness in her voice, her fierceness, doesn't support this. I was aware, suddenly, that she has never cried with me, uncovered her sorrow to me. She hinted at family and marital tensions I was afraid to probe. Am I disappointing her? I sense she is comparing my trauma to her own with her son. I squirm under her scrutiny.

Back at the house my need was immediate—sleep. I grabbed a pillow and quilt for the couch and let exhaustion take over. My palms opened, my breathing evened. When I awoke clouds had moved in, encouraging me to prolong my nap, to burrow back into its delicious relief.

The phone rang, and Paul's voice sang into my heart. Recognizing my fragile spirit, he nourished it with his own strength and love. He will be up here soon. I can see the end of our separation.

The evening with Scott and Alice was simple and quiet, for me thoroughly enjoyable and restorative. Scott prepared a delicious meal of hot sausage and rice. The Cabernet was deep and spicy in its crystal glass. He and I found two upbeat films at the corner video store. The three of us watched them, snuggled together on the couch. By the time I went to bed I was so infused with well-being that I slept a full, deep, uninterrupted five hours.

MONDAY, JUNE 20

Paul arrived in Juneau just in time for me, but as we expected he withdrew almost immediately into his work. He seems to need a lot of sleep, though of course his eagerness to do and see is keener than mine. Our social busyness has significantly limited our time alone, but the flow of love and protectiveness from him is steady and strong. Our return to Seattle together seems significant to me now. I expect it to have the impact of opening a new book, both ending and beginning a new chapter.

The light over Juneau is white and cottony. I sense the heaviness of a low-pressure system, or at least of a weather change. I myself am run down. Fatigue has settled in behind my eyes.

We're eating dinner at Gloria's tonight. A few hours with her family is all I can handle. Allen's mental illness fills me with sadness. There was a time when I could help him, when I could coach him through his English assignments, hike with him, even draw out the confusion in his mind. Now my own confusion stands between us.

I guess I am more hurt than I want to admit that Gloria cannot really help me. She has her own pain. The best I can do is try not to burden her with mine.

TUESDAY, JUNE 21

The beauty of last night's sunset was unbearable. After dinner we drove with Scott and Alice to Outer Point to celebrate the summer solstice and the successful end of Paul's project. We carried our champagne, tape deck, and backsaw over the planked trail to the rocky beach. Wordlessly we gathered wood for the fire. Much laughter as we sipped our drinks, adjusted the blaze, took pictures. All the day's gray overcast had given way to blue sky and wisps of cirrus clouds. The frosted Chilkat range, the south end of Shelter Island, the headlands beyond Lena Point rose from the polished, pale-blue water. An otter splashed, eagles whistled, a porcupine waddled up the beach. None of us wanted to be anywhere else, to have anything more.

The sun set at ten, and the blues turned to pink, then deepened to peach and fuchsia. The water turned to copper.

To my left Scott and Alice had fallen silent. She was tired, ready to leave; Scott was delaying our departure with gentle humor. I lay my head on Paul's thigh, memorizing the moment. The thought of leaving tore at my heart. Would I ever be here, be anywhere like this, again? In the midst of Scott's description of their coming celebration of the Fourth of July I started to cry. Paul caressed my hair and kissed the top of my head. Scott moved to the other side of the fire, next to Alice.

"It's so beautiful," I said. "But I liked it better when I could take it more for granted." Everyone and everything seemed to understand.

Gestures and words restored the light mood. We gathered our gear, killed the fire. Alice and I walked back to the car. We spoke of getting on with living, doing now whatever wonderful things could be done. Back at the house Scott and I sipped iced lime seltzer. I slept marvelously.

Only now am I beginning to understand why the pain surfaces so strongly in the midst of happiness. All my moments of intense joy are braided with those moments of terror. As I appreciate the joy, savor and treasure it, wrapping it carefully for safekeeping, I am reminded of why I must do this. *Look,* the terror says, *I am everywhere. Even here.*

WEDNESDAY, JUNE 22

As soon as our plane rose above the paint-by-number mountaintops and into the clouds, I once again entered a state of transition. Well, I had done it. Made a trip alone, however safe. Survived five days without Paul, Jack, or Margaret. Tested Alaska anchors and found them secure. Found some strength to give my sister. Saw and felt the fierce beauty of Southeast Alaska and looked in the mirror it held up to me. For four years Alaska had challenged my personal resources, humor, and strength. These past eleven days have reminded me of all that Alaska has given me, and I am grateful.

Looking down at the patterned lights of Seattle I sat bolt upright. Somewhere among those lights is the man who almost killed me. Still, Seattle is my home, has been since childhood. I have work to do within myself, and genuine fears to face. Juneau reminded me of my old energy; I saw it in the hopeful eyes of my friends. I want it back. However changed, I want it back.

SATURDAY, JUNE 25

Clearly, the high following my return from Juneau has faded. The past two nights have been ragged, my sleep filled with restless dreams, punctuated by long sleepless spells. I fantasize about trapping the rapist, asleep or awake; occasionally he traps me. The flashbacks are clear, unbidden, unpredictable: the pressure of the sharp blade at my throat, the smoothness of his hand moving between my breasts and down my belly, his voice in my right ear, the hardness of the metal chair against my bare back, his weight on my body. His thumbs pressing into my neck.

I shouldn't be, and am not, surprised. Painful facts and experiences have stepped back into my life. Whereas in Juneau I faced only my interior darkness, here the exterior reminders are everywhere.

"Some of this is over my head," Connie admitted one morning on the phone. "Our Rape Relief training prepares us to work with survivors whose lives have been threatened. But the issues you're raising about being forced to the brink of death would probably be handled better with a professional therapist. We're just volunteers."

So I returned, as I had never expected I would, to the mental-health clinic at Group Health. "Did you think I'd come back?" I asked as I settled myself into the comfortable chair next to Judy Burns's desk. Climbing the circular stairs to her office, I had been only a little nervous. "It's been three months."

Judy merely smiled. "How have you been doing?"

"OK," I answered. "I've been working with a counselor at Seattle Rape Relief, and that's helped a lot. We talk a couple times a week. I guess you had a hunch that's what I needed when you told me about them." Judy nodded, and I went on to describe the trip to Juneau, the work on the boat that Paul and I are doing, the support group that's starting up this week. And my cancer scare.

"Thank god for Connie," I said. "She really helped me get through it, bad enough in itself but even worse when I spotted the man who raped me."

"It was you who made the decision to tell her about the biopsy," Judy pointed out. "You took action when you asked for her help."

"That's true," I said. "But it brought something to the surface that she says she's frankly stumped about. What I felt when I was being strangled is stronger than ever now."

"What was that feeling?"

"It's hard to describe. It wasn't the fear of death, though that was there, of course. It was the reality of *dying*. When I was finally able to think about what that breast lump might mean, I realized why I had been denying it was even there. I didn't want to remember death again. It was so . . . lonely." I stopped and focused my gaze, which had drifted inward, on her face. "And I'm going to have to go through it again."

"Go through what?"

"That . . . loneliness. I've got to die someday, somehow. Will it feel the same? I want to believe that another kind of death will be different. You know, the kind everyone says they hope for, sudden and painless, or at home surrounded by loved ones." I stopped and thought about what I was asking her. "My question can't be answered, can it?"

"It can be asked," she replied. "Others ask, people who face terminal illness, or who've been in near-fatal accidents or in combat. I don't think the answer—if there is one—comes easy. It's work."

This time, I made another appointment before I left.

MONDAY, JUNE 27

The high, warm overcast of the past two days persists. I stumble through jobs: clean the galley, epoxy and scrub the hatch, make some phone calls. Exhaustion and anxiety are catching up with me. Determined, though feeble, I attempt to push through.

Since last week, when *White Cloud* pulled into the marina, Helen and Brad have been neighbors. Most of Saturday she and I talked, through coffee, through my dismantling of the hatch, during dinner prep. We laughed often, though the topics of our conversation were deadly serious: fear, the reactions of friends, our altered sense of ambition, coping. It was comforting to compare notes, to be with someone who believes and feels with me utterly. And whose attention wanders as mine does, hers to the inner threat of her cancer, mine to an exterior, human danger. Neither of us is afraid to talk about these most important events in our lives, or to listen.

It could have been the weight of her pain that, finally, weakened me. Paul noticed it after dinner, before I did. There it was, all right, that heaviness and emptiness below my ribs. These intensified as we walked into downtown Ballard, watched the Cajun band at the Firehouse, stepped into Diane's Pub. I felt isolated, cut off from living. Couples bounced and smiled on the dance floor; a woman laughed as she surrendered her darts and picked up a beer; four men joked, their voices loud and happy over a poker game as the chips were clicked into stacks. Paul and I saw these from the darkness, looking into golden rooms. But it was the subject of the Fourth of July that did it.

For me, the Fourth of July marks the official arrival of summer, the first long gaze into fall. I realized with anguish that time had raced ahead of me.

Then yesterday. It began with a good breakfast and our absorbing chores and jobs. Impulsively, we decided to drop in on Gary and Sandra. Since their visit in late February, which left me exhausted, they have been distant. I don't want to believe that these friends, who for almost ten years partied and sailed and laughed with us, cannot stand by us now. So when Sandra called Friday to ask how we were and to suggest we stop by sometime, I promised myself that I would make the next move.

But from the moment we arrived all was flat and forced. Sandra's hug was too controlled to convey the warmth I used to feel from her. She walked us to the garden, where Gary was meticulously trimming the flower beds that bloomed voluptuously around us. The two of them spoke excitedly about their Seafair party in August: the food, the band, the colors of the paper plates and napkins. I searched their faces for something more. Not one honest expression, not one steady direct gaze. Inevitably I felt that what had happened to me needed to be buried furtively. It was as though I were responsible for the awkwardness.

"Is there anything you want to ask about Migael's attack?" Paul asked abruptly.

Gary and Sandra flinched, as I did. In their eyes I saw a hurried retreat.

All the way home I cried, baffled and hurt. "These are supposed to be my friends!"

Paul shook his head slowly as he drove. "It isn't you," he said, touching my hand. "You haven't done anything to them. For some reason they can't handle it, or us, right now. But it isn't you."

I nodded, accepting Paul's explanation. Someday I may be ready for the kind of friendship Gary and Sandra can offer. For now, I must let them go.

THURSDAY, JUNE 30

Last night's dreams have faded except for a few sharp images: me in a hospital bed, curled on my side, tended by doctors and sheltered by friends; walking through concrete corridors looking for a swimming pool and changing room; an overriding sense of long-term illness.

I lay awake for an hour or more last night. Even hopeful plans offered no escape. It could have been caused by the strawberries and rich cream Paul made for dessert. But most likely it was the aftereffects of my first group session at Seattle Rape Relief.

We sat in a circle of comfortable chairs, the early-evening sun warming the room. My heart was pounding. I was struck by the attractiveness and youthfulness of every woman there. An air of fragility touched everyone—even, very lightly, the three facilitators. The six others, though rigid, sparkled like fired crystal. One clumsy move would have shattered us all.

The wide eyes that met mine were hopeful, timid, and held a terrible knowledge. I was both comforted and horrified. Why would anyone hurt these women? How could it have been permitted? All those numbers represent real humans; we are just a few of them.

This first session was half business, half introduction. We explained what we hoped to gain, learned our names, compiled a list of topics. Experiences and ages clearly vary. I sense I am the oldest, and that my assault is the most recent, but this is only a hunch. The temptation to compare is strong, though as specifics are revealed this soon loses importance.

My overwhelming emotion was of gratitude, for the love and support that has surrounded me from the first day, for all my life experiences and happiness prior to the attack, for my plain good luck. Denial, rejection, blame, were in all their voices. And, until now, repression and withdrawal. Again, these are only first impressions, but they are strong ones.

What a fascinating experience this is going to be!

And a painful one. Until this moment, I now realized, I had felt that I was alone, as though I were the only woman who had ever been raped. I had empathized with every victim in every news item I've encountered since February, but it was *myself* I put into each experience. Now I am faced with living, unique women, each holding her pain closely and fiercely. Each bears a story that she will uncover in her own way, at her own time. Each will say: "This happened to *me*."

So I am understandably weakened today. Conversations and visits with friends helped me maintain my equilibrium, but slowly my footing was disturbed. The noise of the boat traffic on the ship canal rose to a pitch I'd never remembered before. The weekend sailing plans, and the preparation they required, confused me.

This evening Paul works out in the shop, cutting the plywood for our aft-cabin berth. Time alone has calmed me. I am eager for tonight, in bed, when I can wrap myself around Paul and feel completely sheltered, very nearly whole.

9

FLASHBACK

Remember (when time comes) how chaos died
To shape the shining leaf. Then turn, have courage,
Wrap arms and roots together, be convulsed
With grief, and bring back chaos out of shape.
I will be watching then as I watch now.
I will praise darkness now, but then the leaf.

—CONRAD AIKEN

MONDAY, JULY 4

As we sailed north from Ballard on Saturday I could feel the tension slowly loosen its grip. Motoring through the Port Townsend Canal and into Kilitsu Harbor, eyes on the depthsounder, my attention was riveted on the immediate present. This is the level of adventure I choose in my life: a challenge to my senses, intelligence, and experience, with the reassurance of multiple backup systems and the reward of a secure anchorage. Fear, when it arises under these circumstances, is within my limits to face. Confidence-building, strengthening activities.

Two nights at anchor in the silence of Mystery Bay are having the desired effect. I am calmer, my thoughts wander more pleasantly, I feel more energy and independence. I am much less wary. (I was well inside the Port Townsend Safeway yesterday before I realized I was not scanning faces.) I've been happy to cook and have thoroughly enjoyed the country-road walks, breathing in the smell of dry grass, wild roses and cow manure—all smells I associate with childhood well-being.

We head back to Seattle today, hoping to sail most of the way, in no great hurry. Just Paul and me—very nice. Almost like old times, before Alaska, when we thought we'd faced all the challenges Puget Sound could offer and were itching to stretch ourselves to the north. When Seattle represented the safe and the predictable.

The flashbacks of the strangling are strengthening again. Why? Each fragment of that event is emerging, taking shape (and sound and touch and thought) like pieces of a puzzle moving toward one another. When will they form the terrifying whole? Is this the "work" Judy Burns referred to in our last session?

Time to go clamming. A good low tide, high overcast, light winds. Time for rubber boots, gloves, and the clean smell of wet beach. What is *he* doing today? At ease, laughing with friends or family, looking ahead to barbecue or firecrackers? Or is he gearing up for another attack, his mind jumpy, hateful, confused, scared? On Independence Day, 1988.

FRIDAY, JULY 8

After a perfectly normal Tuesday (hooray hooray—Migael is really back in form), and even most of Wednesday, my spirit dipped. Largely, I think, because of the therapeutic measures I am now taking, both group and individual.

Wednesday night's group session began easily enough, but for me disintegrated with the discussion of myths about rape. One of us stood at the flip chart as we talked, listing each myth with bold strokes of a felt-tipped marker: Women ask to be raped; a woman can prevent rape if she wants to; rapists are sex starved. The list grew, and steadily I began to close down in the face of a hard truth: All the myths are alive in this society. We victims are left with a mythless reality that magnifies our isolation and helplessness. What was the point of that exercise? Surely not to organize us into a crusade. I am no more ready to teach the world about rape than a cancer patient is to find a universal cure.

I actually felt I was doing pretty well yesterday, laundry and all (that task is almost routine now in my newfound busy but roomy laundromat). But when Paul got home I clung to him, and his words—that it was "up to me" to decide how long his business trip to Hawaii should be—were unexpectedly devastating. Up to me? I haven't faced his trip to Kodiak at the end of this month, let alone the Hawaii trip in August. His absence, with its overtones of abandonment and enforced solitude, has yet to be "natural" for me. The contrast between me-now and me-then is disheartening.

Napping in Paul's arms calmed me as words could not. But my sleep was erratic. Wednesday night I had dreamed of being followed as I walked with another woman (my sister?) who explained in an academic tone just how I could avoid being attacked, even as the inevitable danger increased. That was followed (hours later when I fell asleep again) by a dream in which I was telling my story to the Wednesday support group. Only a few of the women paid any attention. I talked on compulsively, despite their rejection of me. I cannot remember last night's dreams, though there is no mistaking their ominous tones.

I hoped for some release today in my therapy session with Judy Burns but was disappointed. "Sometimes I think I'm afraid of happiness," I said. "I don't trust it. I may even be avoiding it. Is this the beginning of despair?"

"I don't think so," Judy said from her chair. She sat gracefully, her legs crossed, her shoulders relaxed. "I've never heard you ask 'why me?' or blame yourself for the assault. I never even get the sense that you want to erase the experience from your life. You've accepted the reality of what happened, and it's natural that all your previous assumptions about life, including happiness, are challenged. Shaping new ones is a lengthy process."

Are patience and time the only tools? What is Judy's role? Some of her questions did lead to intriguing revelations: strong associations between the flashbacks of the strangling and water; the anxiety that arises whenever I leave anything familiar. And she had good advice about the support group: Do not attempt to protect it from my experience; get out if it is not helping. Yet what are the early signs that it is helping? Tough to determine, when healing often feels like hurting.

Feeling set adrift, I drove to Stan and Teri's on my way home, hesitating at every turn. I needn't have. Teri gave me the hugs and smiles I needed. "Good for you," she said. "I hope my own clients can turn to friends when their hour with me isn't enough. Quit it, Ben!" She turned abruptly to her three-year-old, who was twisting a toy screwdriver into the coffee table. Jason, his younger brother, chewed happily on a yellow plastic star. They were both grinning. I grinned back, sat on the floor, picked up one of their books. Instantly, the boys were turning the pages with me.

Within a half hour I was back on course. Now, at almost 4:00 P.M., I have been floating quietly for over two hours, in the perfect blue-bright afternoon. The weekend promises to be pleasantly productive. I want to dive into my boat projects, plant myself firmly in the present, and wash myself over and over with ordinary living among good people.

SATURDAY, JULY 16

I might as well face it: I just don't sleep worth a damn on Wednesday nights. Too much gets churned up in that support group, and everyone's emotions are exposed.

Most of last week's session focused on Linda's story. I'm

guessing that she is in her mid-twenties, perhaps a bit older. Her skin is supple and unlined, her eyes round and bright, and she clings fiercely to her independent self despite her profound loneliness and thoughts of suicide. She has been raped twice, the first time by a fellow student. "I'd known him for months," she cried as she spoke. "We had all our classes together. Before he raped me he held a knife to my throat . . . and said he was going to teach me never to trust anyone." Afterward, the friend she turned to for comfort ended up comforting the rapist. "She felt sorry for *him*." Linda managed an ironic smile through her tears. "She was convinced that horrible things were happening in his life which explained— excused, really—what he did to me. She wanted me to try to 'understand' him." Betrayed and abandoned, Linda withdrew from the college, enrolled in another. There, years later, she was raped by one of her professors. She reported it to the school, but the faculty and staff discouraged her from pressing charges. The professor was well known in his field. He had a family. And wasn't she close to getting her engineering degree? Linda shook her head slowly back and forth. "It was as if I was the one who had done something wrong."

Her sobbing filled the room. I wanted to rescue or advise her; of course, I did neither. Her cry was for simple acceptance and belief. The reaction that surprised me was how actively I tried to come up with reasons her assaults would never happen to me, almost as though I were looking for ways she could have prevented them. When I realized what I was doing, I stopped. I had been in those same vulnerable situations, many times. How often had I studied with a male friend in college? How often had I been alone with my professors in their offices? I could remember myself at her age, blameless, bold, and assuming the best of other humans. Everything that happened to Linda could have happened to me.

What Linda's story made me feel most was a deep affinity. Not an affinity for her rapes—hers are so different than mine—but rather an affinity for her suffering. It would seem that suffering, like love, is measureless; it exists or it does not.

When it exists, it is bottomless. The urge to compare experiences, which I had felt through the past two sessions, dissolved. All of us have suffered, each of us differently. Linda is the first to describe, in detail, a rape distinct from the one I know. Four more will be described in the coming weeks.

Paul's sister returned from Europe last week; as soon as Chris emerged from Customs at the airport I realized how much I'd missed her energy. She immediately planned a get-together at the family home on Whidbey Island. We arrived only to discover dry rot around the upstairs toilet and considerable water damage in the downstairs bathroom. Chris looked at Paul and grinned: "Guess my vacation ended just in time." Today the two of them are tearing out walls and ceiling, laughing and groaning at the nests of dead mice and ants that damp space has been harboring for years. Meanwhile, I sit in the sun writing, poking around in my own rot, unable to throw the stench out into the driveway and cart it to the dump. Mine is a process more akin to composting: Over and over I turn each heavy shovelful, working it into the good soil, hopeful that in time the soil will be richer.

TUESDAY, JULY 19

A hot evening on the back deck. Wearing as little as I can and still sweating lightly. Have absolutely no desire to be anywhere else.

Tonight in Atlanta Jesse Jackson delivers his rousing campaign speech. The crowd there—noisy, excited, full of importance—is the exact opposite of us marina liveaboards. Here, only the simplest activities ripple the stillness of the ship canal. On the other dock a neighbor and his buddy putter around in his skiff. Ed leans back in his deck chair in the shade of *Eagle*'s aft deck. Brad and Helen read quietly aboard *White Cloud*. Across from me Paul chats with his mom on the phone. When the sun gets low perhaps we'll walk up the hill to watch the sunset, though already I feel this lazy resolve melting in the heat.

It is for evenings like this that I live on a boat. And never have I appreciated more the feeling of being suspended between activity and introspection, as between water and air.

WEDNESDAY, JULY 20

The technical writing job I was told about last spring has materialized, and yesterday I started working. I am dizzy and excited at the change it has made in me. A new filter has dropped into place, subtly altering every hue. Now a structure overlays my days—I spend four hours every afternoon in a nearby office complex, working with a team of programmers. During these hours I forcibly set aside my random fears and wariness, concentrate instead on explaining how to enter, retrieve, and manipulate data while learning the computer program myself. It is not a huge project, three to four weeks at most, but its impact will be enormous. Already I am thinking ahead whole weeks, fitting all my other activities around those four hours, mindful that I must resist the temptation to crowd myself.

Yet suddenly there seems to be so much to do! The weather has turned splendid, ideal for refinishing *Orca*'s teak trim. Paul has completed the berth in the aft cabin, a perfect opening for me and my sander, fillers, and paint. The companionway and ladder look worse every day. Hold it! Remember the great lesson: Take it easy. Don't get overwhelmed. Take time to heal.

THURSDAY, JULY 21

Another group session last night. Another story. Another day of troubling, shifting reflections.

This time, it was Jody who volunteered. She began by

looking directly at Linda. She fingered her bone necklace; Jody is an anthropologist, and her jewelry always intriguing. "Thank you for going first," she said. "I was afraid I was the only one here who had been raped more than once."

Her first rape occurred when she was a senior in high school. She gave a friendly man she had just met a ride into town. He raped her on the railroad tracks. She told no one. "I figured OK, I've been raped. It's a tough world. Life goes on." A year later, at a party, she was gang-raped. "There was a lot of drinking, and lots of drugs." Jody's large brown eyes grew luminous. "I woke up with parts of my clothing missing, my hair caked with mud, vaguely aware that something horrible had happened to me. Weeks later, I overheard two women who had been there. They kept talking about 'that little thing, with all those men on her.'" Jody was crying now. There was no other sound in the room.

"That was seventeen years ago," she said, wiping her cheeks with her handkerchief. "Seventeen years, and I'm still afraid."

SATURDAY, JULY 23

Breakthrough. Amid yesterday's sun and warmth, after a string of lucky events, I put my finger on Mugshot #4. *He* is in jail, under arrest for his actions on February 9.

I awoke at seven yesterday morning, exhausted by the previous evening's glut of unexpected visits from friends, feeling fragile and close to tears. I was relieved that Chris was ready to come over as soon as I called. Thank god her job as a maintenance carpenter for the city gives her Fridays off. She would be able to help me away from the edge I was teetering on, to get the balance I needed to go to work in the afternoon.

Within minutes of my call to Chris, Detective O'Brien called. I jumped at the sound of his voice, momentarily confused it with Stan's. He and Detective Peters wanted to stop by with some new photos, around 10:30, as soon as they put a photo montage together. "Sure," I said. Oh, Jesus, I thought.

Just over an hour from now. Just like that Friday in March, four months ago, when they came to take my statement.

As before I rushed around in a frenzy to straighten up the boat. I changed from shorts into my jeans. Even considered paying some bills, anything to fill the time. Something was going to happen, at the very least something was developing, and I couldn't predict how I would feel after they left. I made a pot of coffee. I tried to gather up my poise.

Time slowed down as events piled up. Chris arrived, her heart and arms open to me, her eyes kindled by excitement. Brad returned from Lake Washington in our dinghy; no sockeye, but plenty of enthusiasm for my impending meeting with the detectives. Helen's irrepressible smile and giggle quickened with anticipation. My heart raced, my eyes traveled to the gate, my hands twitched. What did the detectives really want?

Brad and Helen left for breakfast, Chris and I sipped coffee on the aft deck. On the other dock Ed locked up *Eagle* and walked to the parking lot, startling in his new jeans and white shirt. I gave up trying to concentrate on anything.

I jumped to my feet as soon as the detectives walked through the gate. Chris and I met them halfway. Introductions for Chris: Don Peters, casually dressed in khaki pants and navy polo shirt, Kelly O'Brien with his fat black three-ring binders. Chris went on to Brad and Helen's boat, and as I led the detectives down the dock and aboard *Orca*, they spoke offhandedly about not raising hopes and how really they just wanted me to check out hairstyles, face shapes, and such. Relieved, I shifted gears and lowered my expectations.

O'Brien sat on the couch near the table, opened his binder, and laid the plastic-coated photo montage in front of me. I did not look at it. As I leaned against the galley counter, with Peters standing on my left, I asked first for an explanation of what the next step would be if I identified my assailant. O'Brien flipped the montage face down, told me about arrest and lineup procedures, and then slowly turned it over again. "Take your time," he said.

First, I looked at the entire montage, waiting for a flash of sandy brown hair. All I saw, everywhere, was dark brown. Twelve photos—front and profile—of six men with dark-brown hair. Disappointed, I looked carefully at the top left set, #1, and then the top right, #4. I'm sure my eyes widened. I forced myself to look at each of the other four sets; my eyes returned immediately to #4.

There he was: the short, slightly upturned nose, the height of his forehead, the spacing of his eyes, his cheekbones, and the way his ears lay against his head. Even his mouth, which I could never have described, I recognized instantly. Most horrible of all, that indifferent, distant gaze.

Recoiling, I pressed my hands together and lifted them to my lips. "I think he's on this page," I said softly through my fingers. Casually, as though he were surprised, O'Brien asked me which one.

"Number four." Bending over the montage, I traced my fingers around that face, imagined a cigarette hanging from the mouth in the right profile. Oh, yes. I backed into the counter, arms folded tight into my stomach.

Though my words were not definitive, my body language certainly was. Of course, they had been watching me intently. It must have been an electrifying moment for them, yet their faces remained composed, unimpressed. They admitted that this was the strongest emotional response they had observed in me. Peters asked me if I could identify the assailant in a lineup. "Absolutely," I replied.

Peters asked me if I'd like to sit down. O'Brien suggested I pour myself a cup of coffee; he was hurriedly filling out a form. I poured some for each of them. They talked between themselves while I walked outside to get my own cup, then inexplicably got involved with helping a boat tie to our dock. Handling a line made me feel strong, but when I ducked back inside and sat in front of that montage I felt very very small.

"His eyes aren't blue," Peters said. "They're hazel."

"It's him," I said, looking up from the two photos that seemed to throb, alive, on the table. "It's him."

A form to sign. And then the rest of it. I had fingered a man arrested earlier in the week in Gilman Park. He had been bothering some children, and a parent had complained to police. The cop on patrol who arrested him noted that he matched the description I had given last March and alerted the detectives. Peters and O'Brien interviewed the man; in their easy, open way, no doubt, they relaxed him into talking about himself. The results were almost too good to be true.

He has been living with and caring for an elderly aunt in Ballard. A loner, he doesn't drive. Walks everywhere. Says he knows about crimes in the neighborhood. Before releasing him O'Brien gave him his card, encouraged him to call if he had any information about child abuse. This morning he calls O'Brien from a pay phone near the Kwik-Kleen. He was doing his laundry.

I have no idea how long our meeting aboard *Orca* took. Chris figures a little under an hour. The two detectives confirmed that Chris would stay, that I wouldn't be alone for the next couple hours, then moved on for their next appointment—with *him*. Their brains were visibly engaged. O'Brien grew quiet, ticking off an inward list, making plans, plotting. Peters thought aloud: "Now the fun begins." I had witnessed, though too close for clear observation, what must be the moment a detective lives for: a case clearly breaks, all the pieces begin to fall into place, and substantive action can be taken. The fun.

As Chris and I watched them leave, shock and fear took hold. The shark returned. I wedged myself into the corner of the couch near the table, poured Bailey's Irish Cream into two shot glasses. Trembling, I went over every detail of the detectives' visit with Chris and, soon after, with Brad and Helen. The flashbacks sharpened: That front-view photo now overlay the image of his face above mine as the point of his knife pierced the skin below my left ear. My breathing shallowed and quickened; Chris coached me into some deep breathing. I talked, then fell silent. We attempted a walk; I got just beyond the marina gate and leaned against Helen and Chris, crying. Back aboard *Orca* I lay under a wool blanket on the couch, shivering despite the day's heat.

Throughout, Chris and Helen and Brad held me, and at the same time bubbled with excitement. "You made their day," said Brad of the detectives. "I'm just so proud of you." Chris thanked me for getting him off the street, making the world safer. I was too empty to feel their relief.

I didn't note the passage of time until 2:30 or so when O'Brien's call jarred me into a new anxiety: lineup at 10:00 A.M. Tuesday. The same hour of the same day of the week as the crime occurred. But this time it will be he who is trapped, he who is watched closely.

Paul arrived with his loving embrace, and a hamburger dinner took shape. A late walk into downtown Ballard awakened my first sense of relief: I didn't need to look for him, fear his sudden appearance around a corner. For the first time in almost six months I could relax my vigilance, if only for a few days.

Deep fatigue set in around 10:00 P.M., yet I barely slept. All night the flashbacks tumbled over one another. His face took form on the inside of my eyelids. Fear pressed me into the bed.

WEDNESDAY, JULY 27

It had been twenty-four weeks, almost to the minute, since his physical presence had riveted my attention. Yesterday, in the warm darkness of the lineup room, I stared openly at the man who raped and nearly killed me.

It was him, without a doubt. All his movements were familiar. The color of his skin had not changed since February. His hair was only slightly longer in back, as though he were overdue for a cut. I had forgotten the thickness of his neck, but there it was just as some part of me knew it to be. The shape and size of his right hand was exactly as I had seen it opening the dryer door. Both his hands mesmerized me, the hands that had gripped, probed, caressed, and strangled. And the sound of his voice resonated true into the very center of my head.

I felt both helpless and strong as I watched the movements of the caged shark. My fear was there, but not panic. The emotion that most surprised me, that grew with each minute, was that of power. He was blinking under the blinding light because of *my* description, because of *my* identification last Friday. And all those people—the detectives jittery with anticipation, the witnesses, and other victims trembling with anxiety—all were assembled partly because of me. I began to feel integrated with the world rather than broken from it, a part of its rhythm. It was as though my heartbeat, long irregular, had been normalized at last. Fresh rich blood pumped through me.

Of course, I was wildly anxious. Waiting for the lineup to begin, I wanted to pay attention to everyone and everything; instead I forced myself to ignore all details that would distract me from my only task: to identify him positively. I deliberately avoided eye contact with the other victims; Helen and Brad, who had driven me downtown, Kari, the legal advocate from Rape Relief, the detectives and other police were my only focus.

Some things I allowed myself to notice. Outside the lineup room the benches were hard and straight. No one was expected to be comfortable there. Inside, the room was twenty-five feet by fifteen feet (Chris had measured it on one of her carpentry assignments) plus the open stage. The hard wooden auditorium chairs recalled to me high-school assemblies and college lectures. Each witness or victim was given a clipboard with two printed pages and a bright yellow pencil sharpened to a long point, with a fresh eraser on the other end. That pencil was the most comforting, pleasing object in the room. Of startling reassurance were the badges on the waists of the detectives, and their pistols holstered in leather near the small of their backs.

Before the lineup began a lieutenant read from the instructions on our clipboards. The advice was simple and expected: Do not speak with other witnesses; try not to show emotion if you see the assailant. He flipped to the second sheet, pointed out the eight stick figures drawn across the page. Put an X over the figure that represents the assailant, the instructions read, and your initials. He hopped onto the stage (no glass, no partition separated it from the rest of us), reviewed the motions the suspects would be requested to do, explained how the spotlights prevented them from seeing us. He circulated among us, asking for phrases we wanted the suspects to repeat. He turned the house lights off.

On the starkly lighted stage were painted foot-high numbers, one through eight, white against flat black. The last two numbers were painted on the door through which the six suspects emerged, brilliant in scarlet overalls, like acolytes at High Mass. It was all a very controlled ritual. Each of us had our prescribed role and rules. The lieutenant presided and directed. The suspects solemnly walked and gestured. One by one they chanted the phrases we had given them: "A slit neck is not a pretty sight." "Where's the alcohol?" "Open the door." "Take the first exit to Seattle." "You're a very lucky woman."

I was the first to be questioned after the men had filed out and the house lights were turned on. Detective O'Brien guided Kari and me into a room barely large enough for a table and three chairs. He gently took the clipboard from me.

"Well?" his face and body asked.

"Number three," I replied firmly. "No question." My hand trembled as I signed the form he passed across the table.

His name is Steven Slater.

SATURDAY, JULY 30

I am filled with an almost inexpressible sadness. A heavy ache spreads and recedes from my lower ribs. I never expected his arrest to make me happy, but I certainly didn't expect this dread.

Twelve hours after the lineup, while Paul was flying to Kodiak on an overnight business trip he couldn't avoid, I sat on Margaret's couch, trying to force myself to make up the bed. Something about the sheets stopped me. How many nights had I slept here on these sheets, afraid to be alone? How many more were ahead of me?

"Are you going to be OK out there?" Margaret asked from the bedroom. "How are you feeling?"

"I don't know how to feel," I said, walking into her room. My eyes were vacant. My shoulders slumped under my thin nightshirt. I sat on the bed next to Margaret and collapsed onto her, crying, "Oh, Margaret. He hurt me so much!"

"You are just so strong," Margaret said, holding me, stroking my hair. "You are so strong."

The bed sagged, and I felt the weight of Jack's hand on the small of my back, working out the sorrow. "Don't try not to cry," he said. I didn't.

Sandwiched between them in bed, my sobs became sighs, my tears slowed and, finally, my breathing softened. We spoke quietly. I rested my hand on Jack's arm, touched Margaret's foot with mine. "I feel so safe," I said as the night's peace settled over us.

I never slept. All the bright red motions of Steven Slater played themselves over and over. Like a double exposure, his movements on the lineup stage and in the laundromat, separated by time, merged in space. I dozed once, woke with a start and a groan, clutched at Margaret and Jack. Thank god for these friends.

I called Detective O'Brien the next morning, as he had asked me to do. He seemed eager to talk. Two other victims had identified Slater at the lineup; their charges would be filed later. The charges for my rape and robbery would hold him for now. The knife I described had not been found, but his gray jacket had stains on it that might be my blood.

"I've got a really good feeling about proving this case," O'Brien said.

Peters joined the conversation from another phone, described his questioning of Slater the night he was arrested. "He almost admitted it," Peters said. "He came so close my toes were curling."

"What about the strangling?" I asked. "Will anything be done with that?"

"It's part of the first-degree rape charge," Peters explained. "He used the threat of bodily harm. But attempted murder would be impossible to prove and would muddy the case. We'd have to prove he *intended* to kill you."

Well, I could see Peters's point. At the same time, I am shaken. The attempt on my life has been set aside, dismissed by the exacting limits of the criminal justice system. My experience has crossed over into another realm, the realm of the *provable*.

The pain continues to resurface. I worked on the computer manual Wednesday and Friday, but was incapacitated on Thursday. Yesterday I held together just long enough to drive to the airport to pick up Paul on his return from Kodiak. Today I broke down on the phone with Chris. The feelings are so sharp and strong. Everything seems so close.

Thankfully, the professional help has rallied around me. Two victim advocates, Maria from the Seattle Police Department, and Kari from Rape Relief, keep me informed about the legal process ahead. Connie calls often to listen and soothe, Judy Burns reassures and strengthens: "It's normal for a lot to come back." And last Wednesday the group session comforted rather than distressed me. I felt connected by the story told that evening, of a rape that had occurred more than ten years ago.

Lisa had been very young, eleven, an exuberant and invincible age. Some of that girlhood was still visible in the businesswoman who sat with us now. She had been raped by a neighbor in his garage. "I didn't understand what was going on," she explained. "I'd never even seen a penis before." What she did understand, perfectly, was that she couldn't tell anyone. No one would believe her; the man was well liked in the neighborhood, and his son was a classmate of hers. If someone had believed her, she knew that her cherished freedoms would then be restricted; it would be like a punishment. She avoided the house where the man lived. Eventually she forgot about the whole incident. Until one evening last spring, when she was reading a novel about a young girl who was raped, much as she was. "I cried for three days," Lisa said, looking at the floor. "Everything came back."

Oh, yes. I could understand that now, as I could not have when the group began. Then I felt I was getting stronger. Now I feel I have dropped all the way back. Of course Lisa had suppressed the memories. She was so young then. I can barely handle my own now, at forty-one.

It is so hard! I miss the buffer of shock I had in February and March, the sense of disbelief and unconnectedness with my body. The rapist, who used to be everywhere for me, now exists in a specific place. He has become as real as he was in that laundromat, his body and his violence once again three dimensional. No longer shadowy, elusive, he is under close scrutiny. He even has a name.

IO

OPEN WOUNDS

For love is not the binding of fair lips
With the soft silk of eyes that look and long,

By Joy, whose ribbon slips,—
But wound with war's hard wire whose stakes are strong;
Bound with the bandage of the arm that drips;
Knit in the webbing of the rifle-thong.

—WILFRED OWEN

MONDAY, AUGUST 1

This morning I am weighed down by sadness. My world seems diminished. At 7:00 A.M. Ed motored out of the ship canal, heading for Hawaii. His departure marks the end of a year I can hardly believe. When Paul and I arrived from Alaska last August, newcomers to the marina, Ed had stepped from his boat and walked to the slip we were aiming for. "Would you like a hand?" he had asked. I had smiled and tossed him a line. Now the slip where *Eagle* moored is empty. I am grateful that Ed was here through the police procedures, thankful for his advice and perspective. But it is not over yet, and I will miss him.

Then, of course, Helen and Brad are also gone; her radiation therapy is over and they have sailed back to Port Townsend. So it's understandable that I should feel less supported, poised as I am on the edge of the criminal justice system. Will justice be served? Will I be protected? Though yesterday afternoon's sail was emotionally strengthening, its effects are already fading. I need informed reassurance, and soon.

Juneau, Alaska
August 1, 1988

Dearest Migael,

If I stay up late enough, I am bound to write sappy notes. This is a brief one. I just want you to know I understand a bit how this lineup business and so on brings back all the anguish of the rape-assault you suffered, and how hard that is to work through. It is of course not a setback but a natural, expected course, and part of finally working through the trauma to happier days.

I understand this as part of the broad understanding of how much pain and ugliness most all humans deal with on some level in their lives. There is so much out there that is reprehensible, scary, and unfathomable about the human condition. It is just wondrous that we are able to generate joy, love, and productive use of our potential at all.

It goes without saying that you and everyone who really cares about you will be living with this for much longer than we want to, but we have no choice. And we are going to continue to generate good times and feelings because that is the triumph of the human spirit.

All this brought on by my staying up late working and gazing for a time at a photo of you and Alice on the deck of *Orca*—happy hour at Sucia Island. Such peace and joy! I'm so proud you've got that in you!

We're with you, and don't expect me to ever be able to gush this kind of stuff on the phone.

Love,
Scott

WEDNESDAY, AUGUST 3

The reassurance I needed on Monday came later that day when Maria called from the police department's Victims Assistance Unit. The first omnibus hearing is scheduled for August 11, when Slater can be expected to plead not guilty and the court will then schedule a second hearing. Thank god he remains in custody. Thank god for some breathing space; my interview with the prosecutors isn't likely to occur until after the omnibus hearings. In the meantime I can turn my attention to rebuilding the delicate structure of my life that was toppled when I stared at that photo over a week ago.

Last night Paul and I walked up to Stan and Teri's for help with my confused reactions to Saturday's Seattle *Times*. In a front-page article the police are accused of keeping silent in order to catch the man now referred to as the Ballard Rapist. I have been unexpectedly distressed by the news coverage. Should the police have warned the community months ago that there was a rapist at large? I find myself recoiling when I am pressed for an opinion, or for details about the case by those who have avoided the subject in the past. Stan and Teri—direct and easy in their roles as counselors—helped me to understand my feelings.

"You know, Migael," said Stan, "you're not just a concerned citizen in this. You're the *victim*, an important witness. This is a case in progress. Neither you nor the police can say anything about all this, or be expected to."

"All the women in my reading group were angry at the

police," Teri put in. We were sitting outside, watching Ballard darken below us as the sun set behind the Olympic Mountains. The boys were already in bed. "I couldn't believe it. I asked them if that meant that unless they are warned they take no precautions." Teri shook her head. "Besides, being careful, or even warned, is no guarantee that it won't happen."

"People don't realize what they're saying," Stan added. "Whether they intend to or not, they're blaming the victim. By implying that a woman warned is impervious to rape, they're in effect saying that if she's raped then *she's* at fault."

I nodded as I sipped my wine from the plastic tumbler. Unwarned, was I careless? Would I have been somewhere else that morning had I known there was a rapist at large? Of course not. There are always rapists at large. I was in a safe place, at a safe time of day. Yet it happened. No wonder the community outrage disturbs me. Why should I—or the police—be considered responsible, however subtly, for my rape?

"There's something else, too," I said. "Even setting aside the reaction to how the case was handled, something else bothers me about the news coverage."

"What you're feeling may be a further loss of control," Stan said. "Your case is out there in the public spotlight for the first time, open to public opinion. The same reporters who are criticizing the police could criticize you. It's natural for you to be worried about that. After all," he went on, "the errors in the newspaper don't exactly inspire confidence. 'Elderly woman,' indeed." He winked, and I had to laugh. The same article that had described me in those words had also described Slater—wrongly—as twenty years old.

That was it, of course. No wonder most rapes are never reported. The unpredictable public scrutiny, the implication of blame, the focus on the suspect that shifts attention away from his victims—all add to our private anguish. And the realization that it is not the rape that is newsworthy, but the rapist and the investigation, is deeply disturbing.

SATURDAY, AUGUST 6

Gary and Sandra's annual Seafair party is well into its ninth hour, yet I do not even feel a tug in its direction. Paul and I have had a peaceful, productive day aboard *Orca*, without a glimmer of the anxiety all those casual acquaintances and the dizzy party pace would have engendered. I simply am not ready for "How've you been?" and "What've you been up to?" over and over from casual friends. I never realized how much energy answering those questions takes. For me, small talk is relaxing only with those who have already allowed and encouraged big talk.

Every day this week I have walked with growing strength toward life. All the thrashings of the shark have subsided; he swims in tight circles now, inside the King County Jail, in downtown Seattle. And though I know there are other sharks still loose, and other dangers besides, with every stroll for the paper or drive up to Safeway I am repossessing Ballard for myself. I no longer rehearse all the words and actions I might take if he suddenly crossed my path. I no longer look for the nearest phone booth, or fantasize about my role in his capture, now two weeks behind me. Tonight, walking with Paul to Gilman Park, where Slater was apprehended, I thought how all of this is beginning to feel safer. Not only do I no longer search every face, open window and car, but I am no longer as tense with the fear that I am being watched myself.

The phone hasn't rung all day. I hesitated only briefly before plunging in to a fairly extensive woodworking project in the aft cabin. Most satisfying of all, I actually accomplished what I'd hoped, and even have the subsequent steps planned for the next two days. Just one week ago this would have been impossible. It is so gratifying to see that, despite a week and a half's emotional setback, I am emerging in better shape than before. This is *so* like physical recovery.

Of course, we have learned from past experience. Cutting way back socially has made a big difference. Getting help from

Stan and Teri last week on the press-coverage issues alleviated much of the anxiety as well. Thursday's Seattle *Times* eased it further, with a report from the chief of police. The public hadn't been notified, he explained, because police weren't sure all the assaults were the work of one man. The age of the victims, the time of day—there were too many discrepancies. The article went on to describe Slater's activities in the park before he was arrested; he'd been asking kids to pose for nude photos, and to steal items from their parents' homes in exchange for beer. His prior convictions were spelled out: assault, theft, an attempted rape. The ambiguities that prompted others to pressure me with questions have been cleared up, at least for now.

I told my story to the support group last week. As always I recalled each detail, every word, thought, and action. I was caught up in the drama of it. My mouth was dry when I finished; the silent belief of those women drained the experience from me completely.

Doubt struggles to live even amid my expanding optimism. Last night an alarming thought leaped up as I was falling asleep. What if no physical evidence links him to me and, with only my testimony, he is acquitted? A terrifying possibility surfaced in a dream that startled me awake: He is released on bail and, knowing I fingered him, seeks me out.

MONDAY, AUGUST 8

8-8-88. An auspicious day to receive a brief, official notice from Victim Compensation. I had applied last February for funds to cover medical expenses arising from my rape. As it turned out I never really needed the money; our health insurance through Paul's job covers everything, even my therapy. What do others do when the bills pile up as they wait for months to be proclaimed an "innocent victim" eligible for benefits? I am reminded of my own good fortune. At the same time I am reminded that I, as much as Steven Slater, am subject to cold scrutiny and judgment.

I have decided to take on another computer documentation project, which will carry me through September, possibly into October. Small as it is, this is the first deliberate decision I've made about my future since February 9. In deciding to continue with technical writing at this time, I am also deciding not to pursue a teaching job this fall. How could I? Teaching is exhausting and demanding under the best of circumstances. With a rape trial on the horizon I would be foolish to consider even looking for such work. So much for my paperwork before February 9: application forms, placement files, classified ads. So much for my idea of returning to public education, and those fleeting thoughts—envy? curiosity?—as I drove by Ballard High School on my way to the laundromat. Am I sad? Perhaps just a little. But almost without a doubt it is the best course for me. So much of my life is in turmoil. Writing, even writing about data-processing procedures, is the kind of activity that is best for me now.

SUNDAY, AUGUST 14

Paul leaves for Hawaii day after tomorrow, for five days. "I'd like to stay on through the weekend," he had said after describing the two days of meetings scheduled in Honolulu. His voice was hesitant, hopeful.

"Do it," I said. His eyes brightened instantly, with excitement for the trip and, I knew, with relief at my response.

In fact, only a tiny spot in my chest tightens at the thought of Paul's absence. I think I am ready for the challenge of filling my days apart from him. It is unlikely that anything new will break in the Slater case. The newspapers will be very quiet. There are a number of *Orca* jobs I can start and complete in Paul's absence. Most important, Jack and Margaret and Chris are available. Brad and Helen have invited me to visit them in Port Townsend. I am securely anchored.

At last Wednesday's group we were asked to think about the ways we have been affected by one another's stories. I'm not sure I can draw conclusions yet. I am still reeling from Elizabeth's. She is the only other woman in the group who reported her rape, and almost everything she described was intertwined with regret or frustration associated with her testimony at the trial. Clearly, it was an ordeal—as bad in many ways, she admitted, as the rape itself. So bad she doubted she would report and testify if she had it to do all over again. At twenty-one, where did she get the courage to keep going then, despite a divorce in progress, despite the demands of a young child, despite spotty support? Did her naïveté protect her? Youth's irrepressible optimism? I am, on the surface, in a position of more strength than she was: I am older, my circumstances more clear-cut, the rapist a stranger rather than an acquaintance. Yet I am truly frightened. The trial Elizabeth endured ended in an acquittal. The one that lies ahead of me could as well. Like surgery, the trial may ultimately help me to heal, but it will hurt, and will require that I trust procedures and professionals I know so little about. The entire experience will be exhausting.

Last night I had a nightmare. I was in a huge building that held both a church and a dance hall, separated by a thick soundproof wall. In one, mourners were gathered, mostly men in their sixties and older. In the other, young, smiling men and women were listening and dancing to loud, happy music. It was my job to move the dead, weightless body of Anna's husband from a table in the dance hall into a coffin, and then into the church. His body was wrapped in a damp shroud, folded in half like pie dough. I carefully unfolded him lengthwise, then grabbed the shroud at his feet, which were protruding, yellow-blue, from the end. At first he seemed weightless, but then his weight increased and I called for help. Two or three dark-suited men grabbed the other end. As we approached the coffin my helpers dropped the body, suddenly repelled by their task. Alone, I set my foot-end down on the floor. The body of a sandy-haired man rolled from the shroud. I quickly covered him with a dark tissue tablecloth. The music wailed, discordant and ragged. I pushed through the crowd into the church, begging for help from the whispering mourners. Their bland faces told me it was *my* job.

THURSDAY, AUGUST 18

Yesterday was bad. I forced myself through the routine of shower and breakfast. I forced myself to work in the aft cabin. As I worked, my lack of enthusiasm and purpose reminded me how fragile I am. Anger and pure hate rose up with the clear image of Steven Slater. I was choked by my sobs. The plywood was streaked with my tears.

I didn't know where to turn. The strength I felt before Paul left for Hawaii had evaporated. Margaret was entertaining an old friend from out of town. I refused to interrupt Jack at work, or Chris. Leaving a message on Stan's answering machine, I worked on, afraid to hope for his response.

I tried to push through. Who needs my suffering? I am tired of it, wearied of dragging it with me everywhere. Surely my friends, and Paul most of all, have had enough.

At 4:00 P.M. I drove to Stan and Teri's, determined to help myself, trusting that someone or something would work. I stepped out of my car into Stan's smiling embrace. Tears standing in my eyes, I waited for a cue from him. "Come on in," he said, guiding me inside. "I don't have to pick up the boys for a little while yet." Gently, skillfully, he probed for my thoughts and feelings. Not good enough.

"Oh, Migael," he said, and with his right hand he reached for me and pulled me toward him on the couch. Gratefully I half fell, half crawled into his lap. I clutched his arm and cried.

It is the way children cry, I think. Totally without inhibition. And the response that works for me is the response that works for a child: close physical contact, caresses, murmurs of comfort. Stan didn't *fix* anything, but as I cried and talked in his arms I could feel the fear, loneliness, and anger move aside, displaced by his love and my trust.

By the time I left his house I felt airy and cleansed, though tension still vibrated inside me. The tension followed me into the Rape Relief office, where it intertwined with that of the others in my group. It grew as Sharon told her story.

The man she met in the park seemed so nice. They played frisbee, talked, eventually went to his house for a beer and talked for hours more on his front porch. "I wasn't about to drink beer with him in his house," Sharon said. "I knew better than that." Just before leaving, she went inside to use the bathroom. When she opened the door into the hall, he raped her.

"I was so angry," she said, quivering with rage. "How could he have done that to me?" She looked around the circle at all of us. No one answered her question. She took a deep breath. "Then I saw the baseball bat. Before I knew it, I hit the picture just over his head. The glass shattered all over—he was cut pretty bad. I kept hitting the walls hard, over and over. I wanted to hit *him*, but I knew if I did I wouldn't stop until he was dead." Sharon's eyes shone brightly, and some of us cheered. How good it felt to hear about someone who had fought back.

His cowering cries finally stopped her, and she threw down the bat and left. A month later she realized she was pregnant. The subsequent abortion led to medical complications she couldn't hide. She told her mother. "She had been raped, too!" Sharon cried into her hands. "It had happened to my mom!"

I looked at her, speechless. I was afraid to look at any of the other women, afraid of the despair I might see there, suddenly overcome with the impossibility of making sense of evil. Without Stan's infusion of comfort I could not have made it through the session.

Confused and exhausted, I drove to Hollywood's Restaurant. Margaret and her friends were laughing and reminiscing, excited by the day and the dinner they had shared. Jack and I sat at opposite ends of the long table, like somber poles. Around us the music and color rotated. His eyes, full of understanding, held mine as I steadied my coffee cup with both hands. He drew deeply on his cigarette. His shoulders sagged. Exhaustion uncovered the troubles he tries to hide: the pressures of his job, grief over his mother's death last fall, the resulting family disputes. In his face I saw a kindred alertness and isolation. And deep weariness.

Afterward, when Jack received a call about a broken compressor and returned to work at the shipyard, I was surprised at my strong impulse to follow him. Yet it was Margaret and her friend who inadvertently dissolved my tension, and in the most wonderful way: irrepressible giggles. Their childhood stories of church camp tickled me into real laughter. I found myself laughing from the same depth that I had been crying from six hours earlier. Like music, their giggling filled me with connectedness and joy. I slept marvelously.

MONDAY, AUGUST 22

Before I saw Paul at the airport last night, brown and bedecked with Hawaiian leis, I was excited, eager, and open. But as always, he arrived filled with his own adventures and, this time, still in another time zone. How different the past five days have been for him. I saw it immediately, and incrementally withdrew. His mind was jumping to the next activity, whereas mine was and still is in the present. Sitting close together in the back seat of Jack's car, even lying in bed, he was farther away than he had been before he arrived. Though I attempted to bring him toward me by telling him everything I have been through in his absence, I could feel him withdraw as I did so. We seemed unable to comfort each other or give each other pleasure. It was as though, trying to kiss, we kept bumping heads.

"I can't do it," I told Paul early this morning. "You leave, and I think I'm strong enough, and then I weaken, and then I break. I can't do it alone."

Paul stopped struggling with his tie and put his arms around me. "Who could?" The tears I had been so close to retreated. "No more trips," he said. "No more trips until after the trial."

The trial has been set for September 19. The news of this caught everyone, I believe, by surprise. Pressure is now on the prosecution to package the case and turn it over to the defense, and, very likely, to file more charges. But I am not at all surprised; a trial is surely more interesting than sitting in jail, and my experience says that Steven Slater likes to watch and wait and take almost careless risks. With a trial he does have a chance.

For me, the news of the trial date is profoundly unsettling because it pushes everything into the foreground and places so many important events in others' hands. The interviews will take place, I expect, with very little warning. Hearings, motions, and procedures will be arranged and postponed endlessly. Doubts will surface. I will be a piece on the board of a game others are playing, whose rules I dimly understand. I don't underestimate my value—I was instrumental in setting it all in motion—but neither do I overestimate it or count on the outcome. He could walk.

FRIDAY, AUGUST 26

It is amazing how important Paul's presence is to me. Knowing he is reachable at any time calms and strengthens me. My walk is bouncier, my actions more controlled and purposeful, my spirit lighter. And his physical love—how potent it is against the fear and isolation, how it infuses me with life.

So I am feeling good these days, accomplishing much and, most important, enjoying even more. Yesterday I made not one call nor filled out a single form regarding February 9. Until next week, when I am interviewed by the prosecutors, life can be normal. I have been given a short reprieve that I must not waste.

Last Wednesday's group session affected me very positively. I have had to wait until today to collect my thoughts, and even now I'm unsure of any conclusion.

The session began with each of us describing what we would say to our rapist, given the opportunity. We moved on to the issues of safety and fear, and finally of trust. Two simple questions were posed. "What does it mean for you to trust someone? Who do you trust?" My first thought was that I could answer easily. I am rich with friendships I trust. I would wait to speak until the very end.

So I listened. Initially, the responses seemed predictable, anecdotal, almost shallow. Yet slowly, the very simplicity became profound. The words were only part of it. As each woman spoke, she changed. Sharon sat forward, brushed back her hair, almost blushed as she talked about her boyfriend. Jody's eyes, always bright, glowed with love for her brother. Elizabeth grew quiet and gentle as she described her little boy. Linda fairly bubbled about her new friends.

It was while Lisa spoke that the pieces tumbled together. Her voice and body exuding pure joy, she talked of trusting herself, of leaving her childhood behind, of embracing the future. Listening, I could barely breathe. I was immobilized, unable to speak. I looked at the faces around me, as though for the first time.

I never answered the question. What could I have added? These five women had strung a necklace, bead by bead; I could almost see it on the floor in front of us, lustrous and warm. And the beads weren't pearls, as I had expected many meetings ago. They were rocks, once jagged and painful, that had been turned over and over again in the pocket until they were worn smooth. The hands that had smoothed each rock were scarred, but they were beautiful and strong. And the necklace glowed with hope.

It was an incredible gift. These women, who had spoken with such anguish about rape and its betrayal, could speak with such joy about trust, which is surely as incomprehensible.

Of course, nothing has been explained or fixed. How could it ever be? But much in me has been strengthened—and comforted.

MONDAY, AUGUST 29

He left. At ten last night, barefoot, distracted, and torn with sobs, Paul walked off the boat.

He had to break sometime. And I always knew that when he did I would have to accept that I am unable to help him. How could he show me his suffering? I saw only the tip of it. All evening long, during dinner with Chris, Jack, and Margaret, he had been restless, drinking heavily and dominating the conversation. "Let's party!" he kept saying, as if he could force the hearty good times to return. Chris joined in the spirit, joined him in his jokes, but Margaret and Jack and I grew quiet. I could tell they were as puzzled as I by Paul's loud behavior.

After they all left I washed dishes and quietly opened up the issue. "Are you angry about something?" I probed, uneasy with the barrier that had risen between us.

At first, Paul spoke of his disappointment with the evening. He had wanted to invite more people and make it a party, something I am still unable to do. I sighed in sympathy as he paged through a catalog. Suddenly he began to cry.

"Oh, honey," I said, walking around the counter and over to the table. I put my arms around him, said nothing.

He buried his face into his folded arms, leaned into the table, and sobbed. I held Paul from behind, trying to encircle him. He did not turn to me. A wave of compassion and love overtook me, and of complete rage. I kneeled on the floor, my head on the table, and looked into his face.

"It's all about control . . ." he began, then stopped. "I want to talk with Jack."

I nodded; clearly I could not help. I promised to call ahead for him. Instantly he was up the ladder and out the hatch. I called him back from the sliding window, reaching for him. He kissed my hand and left.

Love was the only strength and comfort I had in his absence, alone in the darkness for the first time since February 9. It was barely enough. I fortified myself with thoughts of Paul. For the first time he was more in need of support than I was. I can hold on until midnight, I thought, and then call the crisis line at Rape Relief. But midnight passed, and 1:00 A.M. Fear jumped on my lap, searched for a spot to settle. And it was fear not only for myself but for Paul. What if he had reached the limit of his support? What if the comfort he received from Jack was so soothing he would need it all night? What if Paul never came back? I pushed the fear away, roughly, but it persisted in rubbing against me. And every time I thought to myself, *Look what I have done to the person I love*, I forced out the truth: *It is not I who have done this.* The cleansing anger grew.

At 2:00 A.M. Paul returned. He gathered me into his arms and I held tight, soaking the shoulder of his T-shirt with my tears. "I'm so glad you came back," I cried.

Intertwined in bed, Paul spoke of his hours with Jack. They had talked and cried, smoked and laughed. They had put their hard luck and suffering together and pulled out comfort and strength.

What triggered all this? Paul explained: It was the prices in the catalog. Everything was $99.95, or $79.95, or $39.95. Almost a full rounded dollar. Like his support of me had been, he went on. No matter how much he gave, he always felt a nickel short. What he could do for me would never be enough. The realization of his own limits had overwhelmed him.

But he had returned, which in itself was well over a nickel's worth. I absorbed his strength through my skin, down the length of my body. When I awoke to the dawn, I pressed my face, gratefully, to his shoulder.

II

UNDER SIEGE

Part of my life is dead, part sick, and part
Is all on fire within.

—Christina Rosetti

THURSDAY, SEPTEMBER 1

I didn't expect the interview with the prosecutors to affect me
so deeply. What could come up that was new or alarming? I
had prepared questions for weeks, discussed them with Debra
on the phone. "I'm not experienced in criminal law," she kept
saying, but her perspective helped. Remembering Kari's calming presence at the lineup, I arranged for her to be with me as
my advocate. I was determined to come through the interview
informed about the forthcoming legal process.

They were easy to talk to. An aggressive energy made their
eyes shine and their handshakes firm. Vince Marcone is tall,
lean, brown-haired, quick to answer a question or look something up. He took the lead, asking the first questions about my
background. Pam Whitman is very blond, about my size,
quick to laugh. I was reminded of a woman I used to teach

with, whose sweet voice and effusive manner disguised an incredible resolve. I am hoping Whitman is the same.

"Tell us all about it," they said, leaning toward me over their yellow legal pads. We were seated around a large conference table. Carefully, I described the event, action by action, word by word, as completely as I could. They interrupted often with questions: Why did I say that? How long did this or that take? What was I thinking? They were especially interested in the times I looked at Slater before and during the assault, and what I had seen. They spoke often to each other, noting every instance where his words or actions were similar to those used with the other two victims whose assaults he'll be charged with tomorrow.

As always, I had trouble describing the actions just before and during the strangling. More trouble, perhaps, than usual. That point, of course, was when the threat of death became the reality of dying, when the violence slipped from rape to murder, when all the stakes changed. Listening, Kari lowered her head, Whitman flinched and squirmed, Marcone's eyes widened. For a moment I saw and felt right through their professional surface to the horror that perfectly mirrored my own.

They pushed the moment aside, as I am never able to do, and continued their probing questions. Slowly, the sediment was stirred up from the bottom of my spirit. Marcone quickly paged past photos of the laundromat and the montage from which I had picked Slater's photo. Whitman handed me copies of the statements I'd given to police. The incident report, covered with Mike Cristo's bold printing, took me back to those dazed hours sitting at the round table in the police station.

"What can you tell me about *him*?" I asked as the interview was concluding. "Can I know any more than what's in the papers?"

They both shook their heads, and I knew without pressing the point that the less they told me, the more untainted my testimony. Very well.

"You know," I went on, "I described his eyes as blue. I'm told they are hazel. Is that going to be a big issue?"

Whitman spoke up immediately. "There's blue-hazel and brown-hazel," she said. "It shouldn't be a problem."

As Kari and I left the interview, I felt the dread return. Through lunch with Stan and Paul the flashbacks quickened, as though nourished by the fish and chips I ordered. My appetite died abruptly. I couldn't eat at all.

Back home I read an editorial about the case in the Ballard newspaper. "I would've liked to have known that there had been several unsolved attacks, even though there was no clear suspect," it read. "Then I would've known if it was safe to walk home alone in the dark or go to the laundromat alone." When is it ever safe? Friday night's front-page *Times* and even Saturday's paper put the case forward again, with speculation about the investigation and a complete list of Slater's suspected assaults—ten in all. So much pain, condensed and diminished into impersonal, tight journalistic prose. Amazing how details about the other victims hurt: Some of the women escaped; why didn't I? I grab so often for the advice the detectives gave me last March: "Don't let anyone say you did the wrong thing. No one else was there."

I set the newspapers aside and read the copies of my statements to the police that Pam Whitman had given me—the one to Cristo dated February 9, the other to O'Brien in March. Both revealed my disturbed state of mind so clearly it alarmed me. I could not recognize myself in the words, though I remember saying them. Those statements were like snapshots taken long ago, more significant to me for their age and context than for their content.

More than twenty-four hours after the interview with the prosecutors I am still affected. I cried in Paul's arms when he returned from work. I caught myself staring into space last night at the group session, at Hollywood's after, where I met Paul, Jack, and Margaret, and today at work. This is going to be hard. Yesterday I took the first real step toward what the prosecutors see as an inevitable jury trial. For the next month and a half, maybe two, my recovery will be interrupted and stalled. And the outcome, like the violence that set this all in motion, is completely unpredictable.

FRIDAY, SEPTEMBER 9

It made me feel so safe when I saw Ed standing on the dock Wednesday in the morning sun, back from his monthlong cruise. I wanted to hug him or touch him in some way, to verify his reality. A handshake would have been awkward, yet anything more would have seemed somehow intrusive. So instead our faces lit up and his blue eyes sparkled.

We caught up on the last month's events. Hawaii and back—all those hours checking instruments, listening to the engine, staying both alert and relaxed. All that time to read and think. And the conclusion he came to by the time he reached Hawaii was that he wasn't having fun out there, alone. That he wouldn't continue, as planned, to Australia. Finally, the things he can do here, the cruising in the Pacific Northwest, seem more attractive. And the people, he said between his words, more important.

His visit left me a bit unsettled. Though he has returned, he has begun a new chapter in his life. Already he is full of new plans. His month out has left him facing in a new direction, as it should, as he intended it to do. Those of us who stayed behind are still walking the old paths. The difference, though subtle, is startling. I am understanding a little how our own friends may have felt when we returned to Seattle after four years in Alaska, and why some turned away, unable to ride out the discomfort, unable to integrate our change into themselves.

The rape support group met for the last time Wednesday evening, at Lisa's for a potluck. Much laughing and light-hearted talk. Lots of optimism for the future. Great food, but I had no appetite. I was struck instead by the changes in all of us.

Since we began last June, each woman has picked up the random bits of our sessions and begun to weave her own net. In the last month, especially, their accomplishments have emerged. Some, by their smiles, are eager to test, even stretch them a bit. It has been so satisfying for me to observe and help with this process.

But for myself, the past month or more has been a retreat. Though still supported strongly, legal procedures have unraveled my sense of control and desire to get on with living. Weekly, my attention is forced back to February 9 in very specific ways. Today I view evidence, look closely once again at that gray jacket, answer and ask questions. Next week there's a pretrial hearing I may be required to attend. I cannot set the assault aside, though I am getting better at enjoying myself when I do rebound. Sometimes the good feelings linger on a bit. But I am still under siege. I crave the safe corner, the refuge of unquestioned love.

So when talk turned to our group's farewell, I felt, then heard, their attention turn to me. Elizabeth touched my leg and asked me how I was doing. Jody said directly, "I'm worried about what you have yet to go through without us."

"So am I," I said.

MONDAY, SEPTEMBER 12

How is it that an hour and a half can explode to fill an entire day? I stepped out of my own life into the middle of three others' routines; the contrast and, especially, the context left me feeling dizzy, almost stupid.

Last Friday was the evidence viewing. I decided to dress for it, to give them all an idea of how I like to present myself to the world when I have my wits about me. A little armor wouldn't hurt. So I pulled on my khaki slacks, striped oxford shirt, corduroy blazer. It seemed to give me some tensile strength, and it made me feel like I could move—fast—if I had to.

It worked, somewhat. But nothing could prevent the hyperalertness that stiffened me, or the maddening paralysis that recalls the helpless terror.

The ease, openness, and humor of others helped the most. Prosecutor Pam Whitman bubbled over with information as we moved from the county courthouse to the Public Safety Building, she opening the doors, punching the elevator buttons, taking the lead. I slipped in my own questions: Could I observe the next hearing? Should I?

Where the county courthouse is marble and brass, the city's Public Safety Building is linoleum and old steel case furniture; definitely the production end of the justice system. Whitman and I walked right through the waiting area that had held my attention so strongly before the lineup over a month ago. Now my attention was drawn to the glassed-in reception and office areas, and the signs warning that entry was restricted. A buzzer sounded as the door swung open into a wide corridor crowded with lockers and the odd table or chair. I had been there before but had seen it so differently, if at all, after the lineup. Whitman greeted those she knew, softening their faces into smiles. I was struck by how similar her professional style is to mine: friendly, enthusiastic, bright. I recognized the good feeling she left behind in her wake.

Then another doorway and a turn to the right. Detective O'Brien looked up from a computer terminal situated in the hallway. He was just wrapping up some work, so sent us on to get Peters. His fingers returned to the keyboard, his eyes to the screen; he can type.

Another turn to the right past more desks, file cabinets, and boxes. The narrowed hallway branched into offices. There, on the left, were six desks crammed into one small room, the origin and destination of so many of my phone calls since February. Tall windows opened toward the courthouse. A small fan whirred from its perch on a stack of notebooks. I could not have created a more cinematically perfect police department office if I tried.

Detective Peters smiled and rose almost immediately. His

office partner turned to face us and caught Whitman's eye. We were an expected, welcome interruption.

"Pretty fancy office," I remarked from the door. There was no room, or reason, for us to enter.

"This is nothing," said Peters. "You should be here in August, when all six of us are in here." He wove his way toward us in the hall, leaned against the door jamb, both hands in his pockets.

"And the jackhammers are going on the street," added O'Brien, joining us.

So the tone was set, light, almost teasing, as I was guided up a very narrow set of concrete steps and through the barred door to the center of the maze—the evidence room. Through all the twists in order to view the prize.

The evidence room was bare, bright, and big, so different from all the rooms we had threaded through to get there. Chris, familiar with the room through her city job, had described it for me that morning on the phone. It comforted me now to see the white linoleum tile she had laid, the blue baseboards, the yellow walls. A square pillar stood in the center of the room; against it was a table and two chairs, the room's only furniture. All surfaces were hard and echoed our talk.

O'Brien gave the incident number to a man behind the counter, which was barred to the ceiling. I could have recited it with him. Two other men were passing Polaroids of that morning's suicide, casting a cold, appraising look at the results. For some minutes we waited, talking. The banter was interspersed with serious talk: The laundromat owner had confirmed that the utility door was always locked and acknowledged that it could have been easily tripped with a knife; hopeful yet skeptical comments about the bloodwork that would make or break the charge against Slater for a rape last June; speculation about Slater's defense; other cases they were working on. I advanced and retreated into the conversation, an outsider with reason to be there and listen, with the wit but not the distance to relax into the shoptalk. I weakened momentarily, thought of sitting at the bare table, steadied myself instead with my fingers against a garbage can. Yet as the subjects of testimony and rape and sailboarding were volleyed between us I caught the clear message: You are a part of us. We trust you to be strong.

The evidence emerged from a door on the opposite wall, dwarfing the man who pushed the dolly toward the table. Boxes of it, as O'Brien had warned. Large white boxes and brown paper sacks, every one taped securely, every one numbered. Every one, apparently, referenced on yellow flimsy in the fat, black three-ring binder O'Brien flipped open.

I was overwhelmed. So was Whitman, who had only wanted me to identify Slater's jacket. A bit of shuffling by the staff located the appropriate sack. O'Brien peeled off the long strip of tape and inverted it. The gray jacket spilled out.

At first, a shock of disbelief and denial. Those patch pockets over the slash pockets—had I seen them? But I have learned to ride out my first response, which is flight, before drawing conclusions.

O'Brien and Peters laid the jacket face up on the table, examined the pockets and sleeves, pointed out the rips and holes where blood had been removed, too little to type. My eyes flew over it: gray, yes; a faintly blue zipper sewn right up into the ribbed collar, exactly what my peripheral vision had caught. Incredible to recognize so surely details I could not have otherwise recalled. I sorted the snapshots in my mind, compared them with the reality in front of me. Oh, yes.

Without asking, I reached for the sleeve near the cuff and crushed it in my hand. The shock of total recognition and revulsion was immediate. The same ribbed cuff I had gripped over his hard wrist, the same smooth fabric that had encircled me, even the same sound as I crushed the jacket. And the faint smell that rose up as I handled it was powerfully evocative. I didn't have the courage to raise it to my face. Enough.

Whitman was satisfied with my response. O'Brien and Peters, by now familiar with my pattern, said nothing more about the jacket. But they were intrigued by the contents of my purse, which I asked to see after Whitman left. O'Brien gingerly removed each item, touching only at the edges or corners. His discovery that some things had not been finger-printed seemed to quicken his pace and his interest. Suddenly he was seated, filling out lab requests, engrossed in the possi-bility of more evidence.

Then O'Brien pulled the photo of *Orca* from my wallet. We all leaned forward to admire her, floating among the icebergs in Glacier Bay three summers ago. Peters asked me about hull condensation and the Taku winds, and instantly I was 1,200 miles north surrounded by low clouds and cold mountains, then with Peters as he described painting four-plexes for his uncle on Douglas Island beneath Mount Jumbo, then cruising the Inside Passage. Rich, beautiful associations blossomed in the hollow room; for a moment I forgot the boxes and bags.

A handshake and a see-you-later from O'Brien, then Peters rode the elevator down with me, walked me outside to Fourth Avenue. The sun had broken up all the clouds, had trans-formed the day. He talked on, answering all my questions, never rushing me off. Whether he had intended to or not, his interest and remarks were strengthening and encouraging. I left, glad I had handled all this alone. All the gains were mine. As I drove home I was buoyant. I felt massaged, prepared by others for a long, bloody round in the ring.

THURSDAY, SEPTEMBER 15

I knew about today's pretrial hearing—Paul was planning to attend—but what I didn't know until yesterday at 4:30 was that I was supposed to be there. The purpose of this hearing was to determine what evidence would be admissible at trial. I was to stand by in case the judge wanted my testimony regard-ing the procedures used when I identified Slater from the photo montage and in the lineup. Hearing this from Kari when she called from Seattle Rape Relief, my dismay tumbled out in stammering obscenities. Oh, no, I thought. Not yet. Not now. All the beautiful morning, all the satisfaction of working, all dissolved in the crushing fear: to be trapped in the same room with Steven Slater. No matter that the room would be peopled by many who are on my side. My desire to escape danger would be overpowering.

Quickly, I marshaled my forces. Paul would be there, and Chris. At yoga class I mentioned the possible ordeal to Margaret; she said she too would be there, and possibly Jack. I returned to the office, wrote the last chapter of the manual, lined up the work yet to be done just in case I was unable to rebound in time. Did everything I could to prepare for the worst.

Yet hour by hour fear tightened its grip; I could feel it shifting slightly to gain stronger advantage. I began to cry on the drive home. Even lovemaking was no release from the fear. All night long I lay rigid, twitching. Feeling trapped.

Margaret drove me to the courthouse, delivered me to Vince Marcone's office, where Kari was ready to wait with me. His office was bare, stacks of paper and black binders piled on the floor, children's crayoned sketches taped to the walls. It looked as if Marcone had either just moved into his position as prosecutor in the Special Assault Unit, or was preparing to leave. I sat in his desk chair but could not relax into it. Kari attempted to calm me with her open face and quiet Down East voice. Small and frightened, I inhaled her solid, strengthening spirit.

The hearing had not even begun when Paul, Chris, Jack, and Margaret joined us, filling the office. Marcone had asked them to leave the courtroom, not wanting to take a chance on tainting my testimony. My identification of Slater was too critical. Would I be alone, adrift on that stand? Why had I not been warned about this? A tiny seed of distrust in the legal system was planted.

The six of us waited. Paul and the others were eager to talk with Kari, to learn from her how hearings and trials like this go and what might happen. Her experience advocating for other rape victims, observing so many other cases, seemed to relax them. But I couldn't ignore the fact that Steven Slater was sitting in this same building, ready for me to walk into the room.

Noon came, and with it the news that I was not required for the hearing. Maria explained why; she had been in the courtroom for us all those two hours and could give us both a police and victim-assistance perspective. Then the prosecutors burst in, charged, electric. Things were going well, but Whitman dropped an important warning.

"His eyes aren't blue-hazel," she said, looking at me directly. "Eye color *is* going to be a big issue at the trial." I nodded dumbly.

Then the detectives arrived, their bodies and faces relaxed. How different from the prosecutors their style is; but then, their role is to observe and put the puzzle together, and this was not, strictly speaking, their show. Their faces were immediately reassuring in the blur of moving bodies. I was drawn to them instantly. Only later did it occur to me that they might have dropped by the prosecutor's office for my sake.

All of us spilled out into the hall. What a tangled commotion we must have seemed. I asked Peters about evidence; had the lab found any conclusive physical evidence linking Slater to the crime? Peters thumbed through the black binder that seems permanently attached to him or O'Brien and described how he had crawled through the laundromat dumpster last February to retrieve the newspaper Slater had been reading. No word from the lab yet about Slater's fingerprints on that paper, but his face was full of hope.

Maria called later that afternoon from Victims Assistance. All the patience and careful paperwork by the police had paid off: None of the evidence will be suppressed at the trial. But the June rape charge was dropped when the blood test showed that the rapist couldn't be Slater. And the other case—he is also charged with molesting and robbing a seventy-five-year-old woman—will be tried separately from mine. More favorable chances for Slater, unfortunately.

Maria's guess is that a new trial date will now be set for some two weeks away, so after what I hope is a good night's sleep tonight I am grabbing those weeks with both hands and exerting some control. I am going to will the Slater case out of my life. A later trial date gives me a reprieve. Time to focus on myself and my life and the good people in it. Of course, I will be distracted by my forthcoming trial testimony. But I will try very hard to think beyond the trial, beyond the fear.

SUNDAY, SEPTEMBER 18

All my brave, proud words last Thursday did nothing to dispel the dread I carried all day Friday. Woke early that morning, tense with anxiety, and searched over and over in the darkness for the courage to go forward with the trial. Imagined every strengthening face I know, and drew from each all the encouragement I could. It has become a ritual by now.

The deadline for the software manual pulled me through the day. I revised, reviewed, printed, and pasted with a focused energy, never wasting an instant. As long as I was busy I could feel tough and strong. But alone in the car, or at home, tears stood in my eyes, my breathing became labored, I covered my face with my open hands. How could I face Slater, with words my only weapon? He had the power to confuse and shatter me, just as he did seven months ago.

All day I struggled. I pushed through the office celebration marking the completion of the project. I made things happen for the weekend ahead. But the crushing dread increased.

Then, at 8:30 that evening, Detective O'Brien called. The lab had coaxed a clear fingerprint off the folded newspaper, and it was a solid match with Slater's. And the date on the newspaper: February 9, 1988. My voice, which had stammered at the sound of O'Brien's voice, so unexpected on a Friday evening, soared with hope and gratitude. Peters's crawl through the dumpster had been worth it. For the rest of the evening, into the next two days, I was drunk with relief.

SUNDAY, SEPTEMBER 25

This past week never was the reprieve I'd hoped for. Reminders of the tough time ahead kept tumbling together, piling up, with me at the bottom. On Monday, the news from the prosecutors about the new trial date, September 26, and their advice to ignore that date. ("Trials *never* begin on the date shown in a subpoena," Peters had told me in the evidence room. "It's the one day we can safely plan to take off from work.") On Tuesday I received a 7:30 A.M. call from the police department regarding delivery of the trial subpoena; on Wednesday, a call from Whitman to set up my interview with Slater's defense team; on Thursday, a call from Maria at Victims Assistance to gently impress on me the importance of that interview, then my call to Kari at Rape Relief asking for her help; on Friday the subpoena itself, tucked innocently among all our other mail, listing my name with nine others as part of the cast of a drama I cannot avoid. Is it any wonder that I am beginning to withdraw emotionally? Or that nightly I dream of twisted court procedures or cartoonlike conflicts of good against evil?

In all ways I am being prepared for that walk to the witness stand, for that moment when I confront Steven Slater face to face. It is not the only important issue in others' minds, but it is important enough. Daily, friends give me a call or a reassuring hug or calming words. And without any deliberate decision on my part I find I am preparing myself. When food is placed in front of me I eat ravenously, as though against an approaching famine. I am rereading the most strengthening parts of all my favorite poems and prose. I reach out for Paul often, absorbing his love. I am listing small tasks to tackle this week (mend the awning, sweep the workshop, clean out the closet), tasks that will give me a sense of accomplishment and control. And I am lining up mentally each friend, each force on my side.

More and more my eye falls on the courthouse and the jail

when I drive by Seattle's downtown. Very soon that court-house will take on a special significance. I will feel toward it as I do toward any country I have visited, its location on the globe marked forever by my own experience. Is Slater also aware of each subtle shift that moves us closer together? As before, he more than I can control the time of our encounter. Which of us will control the outcome?

TUESDAY, SEPTEMBER 27

Almost no sleep last night. When I slept, I dreamed I was on my back, my arms over my head, smothering in fleece. I awoke gasping for air.

"*Exhausted*," I replied when Judy Burns asked how I was feeling at the beginning of our session today. Her office and especially her soft eyes were calming, but tension was visible in my fidgeting fingers, the set of my mouth, the occasional clenching of my fists. "I feel like I'm swimming upstream. The farther I go the weaker I get. And the rougher the water."

"So you're feeling like a fish?" We both smiled at the comparison. "Well, you're not one. You're not operating from instinct. You have a choice. You can choose *not* to testify. You can back off from this any time."

"Yes," I said, "but knowing it's something I choose to do doesn't make it easier. I know I won't back down. You know it too. What I don't know is where I'm going to find the strength to keep going."

"Where is it coming from now?"

"Well, Paul, of course, and my friends. And the prosecutors and detectives have been incredible, from the very beginning. I've been lucky, haven't I?"

"Don't you think some of that luck is your doing? You ask for the support you need, information or affection or whatever. The strength to do that is coming from you. You're not likely to lose that strength now. It's your pattern. It probably always has been."

"But on the witness stand I'll be alone. It'll be like the assault, all over again. Everything out of my control. I'm afraid of . . . the fear."

"Migael," Judy said, leaning forward in her chair, "you survived the assault. How? Not by controlling *him*. You never controlled *him*. But you controlled yourself. You paid attention. You kept thinking. When one thing didn't work you tried something else, even to the last." She sat back. "What you did to survive then can help you again."

FRIDAY, SEPTEMBER 30

As I knew it would, yesterday's interview with Slater's defense team brought the shark back to full, three-dimensional life. All of my muscles are tense. My pulse races. I am sick with fear.

We began, the prosecutors, Kari and I, with quick questions, answers, and observations. This was the end of their day, and they were energized. Marcone and Whitman, just thirty years old, seem ready to explode with ideas and plans. My case does not appear to discourage them in any way. I sense they are happy to see me and that they are frankly enjoying this one.

In the conference room, Whitman described what she will be showing me in court: the photo montage, the lineup photo, photos of my neck and of the laundromat, his jacket, my purse. I flinched inwardly at each item. Each, I knew, would return me to an experience I did not want to relive.

They continued to advise me: I should direct my answers to the jury as much as possible. I should speak with the conviction that I feel. Be strong, they said between their words. Do not be afraid, even of yourself.

We had been together at most thirty minutes when the defense attorney and her investigator knocked and entered. With only a moment's hesitation Joan Miller, slightly round, a bit unkempt, stepped toward me and offered her hand. Her handshake was perhaps just slightly weaker than mine; her investigator's was limp.

Everyone sat down again (I had never risen), Whitman directly across from me, Kari to my right, Marcone to Kari's right directly across from Miller. Miller did not begin, as I expected, by apologizing for breaking our originally scheduled Monday appointment. Instead, she offered her sympathy for what had happened in February and apologized for bringing up events that must be painful and embarrassing. Embarrassing? I thought of objecting to her choice of words, but remembered Whitman and Marcone's advice: Just answer the questions.

None of her questions were difficult. It is just that she is so difficult to satisfy. Whenever I described anything (his hands, his eyes, his build) she attempted to pile on more qualifying adjectives. My mind leaped ahead, down the path she was attempting to lead me. No, I thought. I will not let her words cover mine, or let her obscure the truth as I remember it. She is not aggressive, but her insistence on imprecision threatens me just as seriously. When she speaks I feel the urge to take up a red pen and make furious deletions. The editing instinct is strong.

As Marcone later pointed out, it is an instinct I can use to advantage in court. Miller opened up issues I can grab and run with, which I was careful not to do yesterday, issues that will increase my credibility with a jury rather than undermine it. And she unwittingly stirred up an important realization about my memory of the event: At the time I was not noting details in order to describe him later. I drew no conclusions about his hair color or his strength or his eyes. Certainly I was not thinking ahead to cross-examination in court. I was operating entirely in the present, groping for the best action or word that would calm him, observing through every sense I dared. I was thinking fast, second to second. Deception and escape were on my mind, not how to entrap him. When I closed my eyes after looking up into his face for a single second (his whole face, not just his eyes, which were in any case fixed above my head), I did not say to myself, *Blue eyes*. But the next thing I saw when I opened my eyes was pure color, the filtered turquoise inside my sweatshirt. Blue—very nearly the last color I ever saw. I saw blue as I struggled, my eyes no doubt popping, in the tightening vice of his hands. I saw blue as I clawed at his fingers, as I ransacked my wits for an escape. I was drowning in blue.

It does not surprise me now that, trembling with shock and relief in Mike Cristo's patrol car, I would answer his question about eye color as I did. Or that the color blue should be impressed so strongly on my memory.

All this from just one routine question! No wonder Marcone remarked that I may have learned more about Miller than she did about me. Of course, the churning, tumbling conclusions are mine, hard labor of my sleepless brain. I'm not convinced they will allay the reasonable doubt of a juror, but if I remembered wrongly one briefly glimpsed detail, then it is understandable and forgivable.

Still, if this issue acquits him I know I will be overwhelmed by a sense of failure. It will not be a rational response, and I will eventually recover from it, but failure will be my strongest feeling. Last night, crying in Paul's arms, I mourned all the victims Slater would then claim. And, eventually, those he would kill.

Despite these stakes I struggle for the courage to continue.

12

THE SECOND ASSAULT

. . . we must fight
Not in the hope of winning but rather of keeping
Something alive . . .

—HENRY REED
"Lessons of the War"

SUNDAY, OCTOBER 2

As Paul and I sailed to Lake Washington yesterday and floated in the dinghy near Seward Park today, I felt suspended in time, gently bobbing between the elements. Warm blue water beneath me, warmer blue sky above; my breathing was deep and even, my mind at rest in the present, and I felt indistinguishable from the beauty and love around me. Appreciate, I told myself over and over. In one week the world may be so different. Even the weather was with me. Gentle, almost limpid sunlight. The heat has lost its summer strength, softened by a thread of coolness. Like myself the entire city took a last deep breath before turning the page into a sharper season.

All of us—the prosecutors, the defense, the subpoenaed witnesses, Steven Slater, and myself—all of us are ready. In our separate ways we wait for a courtroom to open up, for a trial to end so that this next one can begin. It could happen any day this week. It could happen tomorrow.

MONDAY, OCTOBER 3

How changed things look today! Last night I watched the fog settle over the ship canal. The dock lights formed inverted yellow cones. Now all is diffused by low overcast sky. The green of leaf and lawn begins to fade.

It has begun at last, in Judge Howard Kaye's courtroom. Relief, of course, is my first response. Margaret and I laughed a lot on the phone just now; she feels it with me. Soon the dread will settle in, but for the next hour or so I will be coasting.

The clock on the wall here at Stan and Teri's ticks loudly. A fly buzzes around my head. In the basement my laundry is drying. This did not seem like a good week to go to a laundromat. And this is a week when I can be extra easy on myself, in every single way but one. I hear this advice in so many forms: "Take care of Migael," Kari says. "Think only of yourself; others can think of themselves," says Connie. "It's OK to slip all the way back," says Margaret.

I am likely to testify on Wednesday. That is so soon. The ups and downs are just beginning—I want to charge forward, then retreat into a corner. This babbling here results from compulsion rather than reflection. Need to talk with someone, then suddenly I think of something to do, or a question, and then move on without accomplishing much. This is how I was last February and March, when making it through a day was challenge enough. Just the first signs, I suspect, of unavoidable regression. Will I move ever backward, a symmetrical reversal of the healing process I have been through so far? Back through the shock and terror and loneliness, until I am blithely sorting laundry into those three dryers?

FRIDAY, OCTOBER 7

I cannot seem to steady my breathing or my trembling this morning. My body is curled on the windowseat aboard *Orca*, but my mind is pacing the marbled floors of the King County Courthouse, my heart is beating wildly in the witness stand.

Like February 9, October 5 was a dizzying, draining round of anxious, terrifying moments. It began with Pam Whitman and me riding the elevator to the fifth floor of the Public Safety Building, where we waited for Detective O'Brien to emerge from behind the locked door. Together we walked up the concrete steps to the evidence room, paused for the bars to slide apart and admit us, waited for the evidence they hoped would include a shirt I could recognize. O'Brien was more animated than I had ever seen him. His eyes darted over the listed items, his hands flipped the thin pages, his quips were quick and scattered. But his mind was entirely focused. I asked Whitman my questions; she began to prepare me with hers.

Two white cardboard boxes and some brown grocery sacks thumped onto the steel table. A blackened footlocker rested on the dolly. Just a few of Slater's belongings, seized for evidence after his arrest. O'Brien's rubber-gloved hand knifed open the first box. He pulled out the jumbled contents: a sleeping bag, shirts; I saw the broad elastic of a pair of Jockey shorts. Whitman reached into the box and retrieved a small, narrow, soft-bound book. "What's this?" she asked.

"That's one of those bibles Alcoholics Anonymous gives out," O'Brien explained, knifing open the second box. Whitman fanned the pages. The end sheets were covered with notes. I closed my eyes at the sight of Slater's handwriting. My stomach tightened.

"Any of these shirts look familiar?" O'Brien asked.

"No," I said, shaking my head. But the sight of Slater's

clothing strewn about, disordered, was an eerie echo of my own laundry basket eight months ago. And I was struck almost dumb by the tangible evidence of his reality: an ashtray, a photo album, a green backpack. Whitman squealed when she accidentally picked up his orthodontic retainer ("That's why we always wear gloves," O'Brien said, grinning). So many signs that Steven Slater was close by. Fear gripped me from behind, but my resolve strengthened.

Whitman picked up the sealed sacks she needed containing my sweatshirt and my purse, handed me the sack containing his jacket. Arrangements were made to bring over the fingerprinted newspaper later. The three of us descended in the elevator to Fourth Avenue. Two other men joined us. Whitman greeted one, O'Brien introduced the other as Lieutenant Lawrence. I shook his hand, looked directly into his eyes that smiled behind aviator-style glasses. "Slater goes up today," O'Brien said simply. Lawrence looked at Whitman and me and nodded.

Whitman and I took the stairs up to her office on the fifth floor, she explaining and preparing me every second, talking fast. Kari now joined us, and Whitman went over the entire examination she had prepared, showed me all the eight-by-ten glossies I would see during testimony (with the pointed exception of the montage and lineup, which I was to see in court) and a huge map of Ballard mounted on white cardboard. Each question, each photo led me closer to the laundromat and to Steven Slater.

Vince Marcone dropped in, asked how I was feeling. "Determined," I replied. After a few encouraging words he left, distracted and energized by the opening statement he would give. Whitman left, loaded down with binders and bags. Kari followed with the Ballard map. Paul arrived, and Detective Peters. Their eyes were dancing with excitement.

"How do you like her credibility outfit?" Paul asked. Already I had received joking comments about my sensible black pumps and tweed skirt.

Peters rocked back and laughed. "You don't need to worry

about her credibility," he said. "Don't even think about that. Someone like Migael is sent to us from heaven."

I smiled, momentarily relaxed by the compliment. "Nonetheless," I countered, "even a witness from heaven has to dress carefully. I bet the jury would have a harder time believing me if I was wearing a tight polka-dot dress and bright pink gloves." I rubbed the pin on the lapel of my camel's hair jacket, as if for luck.

It seemed that suddenly everyone disappeared. The offices around us fell silent as court sessions began. Kari and I walked across the street for nylons (she had developed a run) and a muffin (for me), then returned to Whitman's office where Kari sketched the layout of the courtroom. To familiarize me further she led me upstairs into a room that is a mirror image of Judge Kaye's. I sat with her on the hard bench until my breathing was normal. I looked at the pale lemony walls, sensed the room's volume, noted the distance to the exposed witness stand and its closeness to the jury box.

Another spell in Whitman's office, and then the real wait, on the wooden bench in the hall. The marble floors and walls magnified Marcone's voice from within the courtroom. My hands went damp and cold. Inside I felt a fearful determination that was vaguely familiar; I had felt something like this on the boat over a year ago, the night before we attempted to cross Hecate Straits. Well, I thought, I can function with this.

The doors opened, and Whitman beckoned us in. Kari's hand was on my left shoulder and Whitman's on my right as they guided me in. My eyes passed over the dear faces I knew, then fixed on the path to the witness stand. All eyes were on me, but all my fear was focused on the back of one man. His head turned to the left as I approached. Passing between him and the guard, looking straight ahead, I stepped cautiously up to the bench. My hand grazed the railing in front of the jurors. I looked up at the judge.

His voice was calm and kind as he swore me in, his face brown and lined, his curly hair grizzled. Puppetlike, I raised my right hand, answered to the oath. I recognized immediately that I was in shock and dangerously suggestible. Be careful, I thought. With quivering slowness I lowered myself into the chair. Without even a low railing in front of me, I felt at once completely exposed and unprotected. I raised my eyes. I looked Slater full in the face.

He was at most fifteen feet away. His hair was combed and trimmed exactly as it had been on February 9. He wore a gray sweater, a striped tie, and a pale shirt. His partially clenched hands lay side by side in front of him on the table, and his mouth was tightly closed. He sat rigid, immobile, just as I had remembered. His eyes locked on mine, flickered aside, returned; save for the slightest twitch of his eyebrows, his expression never changed.

In an astonishing reversal *I was looking down at him*. The shock and fear moved a little to the side. A dull rage expanded to fill the space. His mass diminished slightly. And I remembered to breathe.

Beyond him I saw Chris, Margaret, Jack, and Paul, their faces open and giving, in complete contrast to Slater's. There were other faces as well, but I did not see them clearly. Turning my head to the left, I saw Detective Peters observing me as unobtrusively and completely as he had last March when he took my statement and again in July when I picked Slater from the photo montage. At his right Marcone looked back at me through his glasses, then down at his papers again. Between us was a court officer shuffling papers and pads, and a stenographer, blond, curly headed, poised to begin his work. Just below my chin was a microphone.

Turning to my right I faced the jury. They were a mix of ages, sexes, and colors. Some looked back at me. One, an older woman, stared with round eyes. A black man at the far end of the first row turned his head away. A blond woman in the second row looked at me forthrightly. Immediately to my right, so close I could touch her, a brown-haired woman met my wandering gaze with soft eyes.

Whitman eased me into the process with questions about myself. Then, immediately, she took me back to Tuesday,

February 9. Why did I remember that day? What was I doing that morning? What did I buy at Safeway? Quickly she drew out all the detail of my mind, establishing for the jury just how thorough my memory is. Fact upon fact upon fact. She gave me a red pen and asked me to mark the location of the laundromat on the map. I identified each photo she handed to me, then stood up and pointed out details for the jury. Detail after detail. Which washers did I use? Exactly where and how was he sitting? How long did I look at him then? And then?

I struggled between fear and determination. I knew that with every clear answer, with every confident identification of him as the man I was describing, the silent rage inside Steven Slater was growing. All the glowing coals of his spirit were being steadily fanned by my words, just as my quick busy gestures had fanned them eight months earlier. Was I the only one aware of this? Could anyone else see the swelling hate in the calm man sitting at the table?

A question from Whitman. An answer from me. I remembered Ed's advice: Develop a pause before you speak. Every bit of me concentrated on Whitman's question, then every bit of me reflected before answering. And always the internal warnings: Be careful. Be truthful.

All of me was screaming in alarm; so it must feel to a rabbit frozen in the glare of approaching headlights. Yet my mind was functioning completely and very rapidly. And my spirit was rock solid; no one could shake my fierce stance. What I knew I knew absolutely.

Whitman seemed aware of this tension and played it to advantage. Sometimes she blocked my view of Slater, sometimes she pointed him out, forcing me to look at him. I tried to speak to the jury as often as possible; if I forgot, she would move or gesture toward them. She seemed to exploit simultaneously my ease at public speaking and my terror at even breathing in the same room with Slater. Was this contrast as evident to others as it was to me? My voice ranged from calm to quivering, from a confident ring to a terrified whisper. My hands trembled as I lifted the tiny paper cup of water to my lips whenever the judge suggested I pause and drink (he, thank god, watched me closely, watched over me). They trembled again when, overcome by fear and exhaustion, I raised them with open fingers to cover my face.

Detail after detail. Whitman scissored open three of the evidence bags. From the first I pulled out Slater's jacket, slowly and reluctantly. Though Whitman took it from me almost immediately, it was in my lap too long. My purse had the opposite effect; I may have smiled as I fingered the hand-tooled designs. And I clutched my sweatshirt eagerly, recalling instantly all my halibut-fishing adventures.

Question after question. Whitman interrupted often to offer evidence. Joan Miller occasionally interrupted with an objection or request. At every opportunity Whitman asked, "Is this the man you saw? Is this the man who raped you? Could another man look just like him with blue eyes?" And every time my answer was unfailingly the same: It is him, beyond any doubt. It is him.

Time telescoped. What I thought took over an hour took only thirty-five minutes. Yet time raced when Kari and I waited in the hall while the man who found my purse in his garage testified. There were moments when time stopped altogether: as I walked from the stand directly toward Slater; as I stared at the big glossy photo of the metal chairs stacked in the utility room, spotted brightly with my blood; as I described the rape and especially the strangling; and most especially when Slater rose to put on the gray jacket at Whitman's request. His gestures were easy and natural as he settled it over his shoulders. When he looked up at me I froze and gasped. My god, I thought, reeling in horror and flashback. What a brilliant move on Whitman's part.

Periodically Judge Kaye would suggest a general stretch; though too weak to stand, I appreciated the reprieve. Twice he called actual breaks. The encouraging faces that surrounded me then primed me for the next round. O'Brien and Peters hovered briefly as I waited with Paul and Kari after the lunch break. From them I absorbed all the confidence their faces showed me. From Kari I absorbed quiet, gentle strength. And from Paul I absorbed love.

Cross-examination was no harder than I feared, but certainly no easier. Miller's questions were so vague, so unexpected. And so very treacherous. I was particularly cautious when she offered an answer to her own question—where would she go with it? Where was she leading me? Over and over she probed, attempting to find a tiny crack in which to drive a wedge of doubt. But I refused to change what I remembered. How could I? If I had made a mistake in identifying Slater's eye color, so be it. Whitman had uncovered explanations for that already. I knew that if I retracted, even on my one mistake, then everything would be in doubt. Though Miller's questions wore me down and I wanted desperately to stop them, I would not budge. By holding to the truth as I remembered it I would not contradict myself, nor could I be backed, however gently, into a corner.

So I held fast. It was for this that I had been preparing myself since the arrest in July. I knew Slater was my assailant; my job now was to convince the jury not only that I was certain but that I could be trusted to tell the truth. No one expected me to be infallible. They required that I be credible.

Exhaustion must have been plain on my face by the end of the first day, and certainly the jury was wearying, when the judge asked if my schedule permitted me to return in the morning. So politely phrased, and so deeply appreciated.

And helpful to the case. Time away from the courtroom gave me added strength. Whitman came up with some additional points for rebuttal, and I did as well. So the final round went smoothly but for Miller's last question: Why did I tell Officer Cristo the eyes were blue? I nearly stammered as I recalled how I had sat doubled over in his patrol car, remembering that face. Blue—the color that filled my mind then, and colors all my recollection even now. Blue everywhere: my laundry basket, my jeans and sweatshirt, a tint in this gray jacket, the trim and awnings of the boat shop across the street, the seat of the patrol car. I held my breath, lowered my head, and suddenly I was behind the dryers, my neck clenched in Slater's powerful hands, my fingers clawing at his, all of me struggling, dying and desperate to live. Struck dumb on the stand, I felt everything I felt then. I raised my eyes to Miller's and answered, "Because it was what I remembered." It was all I could say.

Whitman ended on a strong note, and I stepped down for the last time, steadying myself as always on the railing of the jury box. I felt numb and empty and very small. Paul was right behind me, and Margaret, and Whitman. Detective O'Brien was sitting on the bench in the corridor; he rose and, after a quick glance and nod my way, followed Whitman into the courtroom as the next witness. I leaned into Paul's embrace.

"I'm ready to go home," I said. "I'm ready to change into my jeans."

SATURDAY, OCTOBER 8

Two days after giving testimony feels so much like the two days after the assault, without the numbing effects of shock.

At 3:30 this morning I woke as from an unremembered nightmare. Beside me Paul breathed deeply in the darkness. I carefully crawled over him, walked to the head, shook an aspirin out of the bottle and swallowed it down with cold water. Through the round porthole I could see *Eagle* reflected perfectly, upside down, in the black water. Intrigued by the sight, I threw on my robe and walked softly back to the pilothouse.

The ship canal lay still and flat; the boats glowed in the low fog, joined at the waterline with their inverted mirror images. All was hushed, tranquil, beautiful.

In the still water I saw with complete clarity the moist eyes of my beloved friends in the courtroom gallery. Then all was obscured and scattered by the frenzied thrashings of Steven

Slater, raging from the exact center of the courtroom. Waves broke against the walls, over the jury box and judge's bench. All order and goodness was overwhelmed.

Bending at the waist, I pressed my face into the pilothouse cushion and began to cry. So many have suffered for me.

Paul stirred, walked sleepily from bed, embraced me gently from behind. "Come to bed," he murmured, stroking my back. "Don't cry up here alone."

"Please don't leave me alone," I begged, turning to him.

Paul guided me back to bed, lifted me up and climbed in next to me. I was limp, shaking with sobs, my face and hair smeared with tears. He held me close.

By the time the pain subsided a gray light was visible through the portholes. When I twisted out of my robe and settled back into Paul's arms a wave of desire rose over us both. We made love softly, breathlessly. My orgasm was like a flower opening to the dawn; at Paul's I wept with joy. "That was for the world," I whispered, "for the entire good world."

We slept until nine, though my sleep was shallow. When I sat up to take the cup of coffee Paul had poured I felt the dull pain returning. I struggled to shower, to dress, to begin a day I dreaded.

So it continued, for hours. I pulled a blanket over me on the couch and gave myself over to the sorrow and anguish. Connie arrived to give Paul a break. Anna called and cried with me. Outside, the fog thickened.

Hoping to relax me, Paul suggested a walk to the corner deli for a newspaper. Each step was slow and deliberate, as though I were wounded. Back aboard, Paul made me a cup of tea. I opened the paper and my eye fell on the headline. WRONG MAN BEING TRIED FOR RAPE, SAYS DEFENSE. Oh, god.

FRIDAY, OCTOBER 14

Last Monday's courtroom drama was every bit as terrifying as the previous Wednesday's and Thursday's, though I was not the central figure. Paul and I were almost the first to arrive. We sat in front at the far end, where I could view the jury; we soon moved back at Whitman's suggestion ("I want their attention on me, not you," she explained). Singly, or in pairs, people entered, took their places. An older man with a kind face introduced himself as the owner of the laundromat and pressed my hands sympathetically in his. Everyone in the gallery benches spoke in hushed tones. Most were familiar faces. Only the recorder, clerk, bailiff, and the three attorneys talked or gestured with ease.

I had missed so much from the witness stand. The tables used by the prosecution and the defense were joined to form an L. I had thought them separate, either because my view was obscured or I had been unable to focus on anything between Slater's face, frightening and frozen, and Peters's farther to the left, so calming and relaxed. The floor I now saw for the first time: dark green with yellow streaks. I had never noticed the frieze behind the judge's bench, or the flags. And the bailiff; how could I have missed such a great-looking blond surfer?

The benches had filled around us by the time the guard brought in Slater. At the sound of the handcuffs unsnapping I jumped and looked up. He was standing, looking in my direction, though not at me, regarding me if at all with his peripheral vision exactly as he had in the laundromat. He rubbed his wrists briskly, then pulled out his chair and sat down. I froze with fear at these natural, unrestrained movements. Paul sat to my right, Kari to my left, but he was so close, so dangerous, so unpredictable. And the guard was so far away.

"Breathe, Migael," Kari reminded me.

Judge Kaye's entrance distracted me, and I tried to contain my panic as he read the instructions to the jury. But the seriousness of the charges, interlaced with my name—Migael Monica Scherer—and spoken in such formal tones, increased the panic. I wanted to explode into flight or rage.

Then Detective Peters walked across the room, briefly blotting out Slater's form as he passed between us. My eyes followed him as he sat next to Whitman, in left profile to us. Instantly my blood pressure dropped. My heart slowed and my breathing evened. There was the piece I had missed. There was the final anchor I needed.

Whitman's closing statement both fascinated and troubled me. She reviewed the entire crime, emphasizing its most horrifying aspects. She led the jury through the evidence, showed them photos at critical moments, refreshed their memories, mentioned my name often and pointed me out many times. Even more often she pointed out the defendant, Steven Slater, who sat quietly. He leaned forward slightly as she spoke, as though his interest were aroused; he rested his chin on his right hand. His sandy-colored hair reflected the light, and his right ear and the skin on the right side of his neck were all I could see of his face. That view was chilling enough.

Then came Miller's closing statement for the defense. Her reference to the "phantom rapist" and the "cloak of innocence" confused me. It was hard to listen to her defense of Slater and criticism of me. I was close to tears when the judge called a break.

Everyone but me stood up, moved around. Kari brought me a cup of water. Whitman brightened at my praise. I described to Peters how his entrance had affected me; he laughed and brushed my hand, which was gripping the bench in front of me, with his. His hand was cool and smooth. I glanced down the bench toward Jack; at the sight of my face he scooted over next to me, held my hand, said nothing.

Marcone's closing statement was long awaited and satisfying. Item by item, he emphasized how completely I had described my assailant. There Slater sat, living testimony of every detail I remembered except one; Whitman had outlined these carefully in her closing, now Marcone was underscoring each in his. I saw several jurors nod and smile slightly, but when he slapped Slater's photo in the center of the bull's-eye he had drawn, they all flinched. My heart jumped.

The trial ended formally, abruptly. I watched deliberately as the guard clicked on the handcuffs, ratcheting them firmly to the bones of those hard wrists. My last view of Steven Slater was his left profile; he glanced at his father and sister, lips upturned slightly. He raised and then dropped his eyebrows, as if giving them a hope he did not quite believe himself. This simple gesture is the only visible sign of humanity I can recall about him; somehow it made the sight of his restraints all the more satisfying to me. The outcome of this trial was not yet known, but at least I could never be robbed of the memory of those hands helpless in cuffs.

It was some minutes before I could stand and walk from the courtroom. Friends came toward me. No one offered an opinion on the verdict, though Kari guessed it would be some hours away. I said what I was feeling: that it had all been worth it. Slater had been off the streets for over two months, but just as important, the legal proceedings had demonstrated a public outrage against him. From the beginning so many people had believed me. Of the jury I prayed: Make them wise.

As we left the courtroom in a group, my eyes filled with tears. Paul moved in to hold me. Kari asked a question that revived me. I groped for the handkerchief in my right pocket; it was the first time I had used it since the trial began. Only now, when it was all over and my work completely done, could I afford to cry publicly.

The hours that followed were full but very slow. Paul, Jack, and I stretched out lunch before going home. When the call did come, near 3:00 P.M., I was brushing my teeth. My heart plummeted with fear at the sound of the phone. Kari gave me the verdict: GUILTY. I burst into tears.

Paul was immediately energized. He rowed over to Ed to spread the good news, wanted to call everyone, quickly put together a celebration at Lombardi's. It all fell together beautifully. The faces of my friends were now smiling. Their eyes were sparkling. Their voices were lively. It made me so happy to see them lighthearted. It made me so happy to feel lighthearted myself.

Seattle, Washington
October 1988

Migael,

As I drove away from Lombardi's restaurant after
toasting the conviction, what came over my radio was
the song, "Stand by Me." Tears so long held back
flowed freely. How right, I thought—after being among
you and your friends, after feeling such strong bonds
between you. Thank you, Migael. Thank you for
surviving, for telling and retelling how you survived.

I am sorry that what happened to you was the reason
for our meeting. I am glad, though, for our friendship.

You stand by me every day. Your courage gives me
courage—every day. No kidding. You were great!

With infinite respect,
Kari

WEDNESDAY, OCTOBER 19

Since Sunday evening, when Paul and I did nothing more than
read and talk, silence and coziness have soothed my spirit. All I
want these days is to putter at home, to read, to reflect, to
write. I crave the ordinary and the routine.

So much has changed. The dread is gone; not the wariness or
vulnerability—if anything I feel smaller than ever—but the
cold, inescapable dread. No longer am I hoarding strength
against that final ordeal, as I now realize I have been doing
since February. The responsibility I shouldered when I called
911 has been fulfilled. What little remains to be done—a letter
and perhaps words to the judge regarding sentencing—does
not alarm me yet. I have been through the worst.

I am sleeping deeply and long. Not since last weekend have I
dreamed of Steven Slater, who in that dream looked at me
across a large table with kaleidoscopic blue eyes. I admit to
waking intermittently; usually his face is foremost in my
mind. But the actual sleep has such restorative power.

Last week Slater pleaded guilty to burglarizing the seventy-five-year-old woman in north Ballard and now faces a stiffer sentence. The news, coming so soon after his conviction for my rape, infused me with energy. I immediately wrote a letter to the *Times* editors, protesting their coverage of the trial. Why had the reporter emphasized my single mistake about Slater's eye color? Why did she seem to take his side? Doesn't she realize such coverage discourages other victims from reporting and testifying?

Next, I sent balloons to O'Brien and Peters, tickled at the prospect of two blue-and-gray balloon bouquets floating in their cramped office. Over the weekend Paul and I cleaned our diesel stove, ridding it of a year's soot, preparing it for the coming winter.

This week my goals have been modest. I have done a little boat work and a little editing work each day. I have performed the routines of shopping and laundry as routines. I have cooked real meals; nothing spectacular or even particularly delicious, but meals nonetheless. Fingering through my recipe file last night, I remembered with pleasure how much fun cooking could be.

Mostly, I have succeeded in achieving a certain peace. I realize it is somewhat artificial, considering the rarefied world I and others have created for me these days. A major crisis or even a moderate challenge could take me all the way back right now. And perhaps what I am feeling is not true peace but only satisfaction—with the criminal justice system, with everyone who helped me, with myself.

TUESDAY, OCTOBER 25

I feel myself slipping today. My attention wanders, my concentration stalls.

I first noticed this at breakfast with my mother. She spoke softly during coffee and waffles at the Salmon Bay Café. "Your father and I are so proud of you," she said. "We followed the trial in the newspaper and on TV. Chris called every day to tell us how brave you were."

"What did she say about my testimony?" I asked.

"She said she had seen your pain before," my mother explained. "But at the trial . . . she felt it."

That was me, I thought, remembering everything. I felt gratitude again for my friends, then guilt that I had asked my parents to stay away from the trial. They had offered to attend, but I knew my father's presence in the courtroom would be difficult for me. "You can't afford to worry about how your testimony is going to affect him," Judy Burns had said. "The fact that he asked if they could attend means that he'll accept your answer either way and understand." Looking at my mother, I clearly saw the anguish it had cost her to keep the distance I needed, and the love that had given her the strength to do so.

I returned to the boat and read from beginning to end the notebook my friends had put together for me. "Testimony is not to be discussed with Migael throughout the length of the trial," Chris had typed on the first page. "This book will allow us to express our impressions to her in the meantime." I thought I would be most interested in the facts of the case as they had been revealed, but reading the handwriting of my friends, I was drawn instead to their personal observations. "Jailer and Slater arrive. Is he that short?" "Slater has a new shirt and sweater. He appears happier. I can see through his disguise!" "I'm sitting next to a very nervous, pretty blond woman. Turns out she's Slater's sister." "What color is hazel, for Christ's sake?" "This is pink-and-red day for our women attorneys. Whitman is wearing her mother's rose-red suit." "Migael, there are eleven of us in here. Your cheering squad. A strong block—a jury of your peers."

Before memory fades, I must recapture the highlight of last week, my meeting with Lucy Gilbertson, in her tiny house in the north end of Ballard. It was in this house Steven Slater robbed and molested her last May. She had contacted me through Pam Whitman. "This very sweet seventy-five-year-old woman would like to talk with you," Whitman had written when she sent Lucy's phone number. "But this is completely up to you." I couldn't resist.

Lucy was at the door almost as soon as I got out of the car. To her left a large red sign, BEWARE OF THE DOG, warned of an animal that did not exist. She was dressed as I expected: a flowered print dress, low shoes. Her eyes twinkled with curiosity and eagerness. Her gray hair was swept up in waves from a center part. As I stepped into her house she took the daisies I brought and gave me a hug. I warmed to her immediately; widowed and alone, yet she had found the courage to seek me out.

Her house was as much a piece of work as she was. Every surface gleamed and proudly displayed as many ceramic figures, dishes, and vases as could be arranged without crowding. Figures beamed up at me from under the glass-topped coffee table. On the mantel two turquoise swans faced each other, flanked by matching low vases filled with silk flowers. In front of the fireplace a foot-tall Snow White smiled over seven dwarfs, each perched on pedestals that branched across the hearth. I sat on the couch, right next to the door. Glass shelves behind Lucy's chair separated the living and dining rooms. These too held surfaces covered with figurines. On the low credenza against the wall to my right was a telephone and a clear glass jar one-quarter full of sugared gumdrops.

She brought me a cup of coffee and a plate of chocolate cake with chocolate icing. She sat down, ignored the food, and opened up. "This is what happened to me," she said.

"He broke into my house while I was sound asleep, through the basement. Must have kicked right through the two bolts on the hall door. You can see where the screws pulled out of the door trim." She shook her head and shuddered. "I didn't hear any noise, must have been sleeping soundly. He woke me up with a flashlight in my face. I tell you, kid, I was scared."

Jesus, I thought, he wanted her awake. Of course.

What he did to this gentle lady was different from what he did to me, but the parallels were chilling. I leaned forward, clutching my coffee cup, as she described how he had tucked her in tightly, pulled a pillow slip off her pillow, and filled it with everything he thought was valuable. He lay on top of her ("He was flat as could be," she explained), fondled her breasts, encircled her throat with his hands and—I swallowed—caressed it with his thumbs. "Do you believe in God?" she had asked at that moment. "You bet I do!" he had replied.

"He made me remove my rings," Lucy continued. "I've had that wedding ring on since I was married, and I sure miss it." She sighed. "But he didn't take the crucifix from around my neck. 'Is that gold?' he asked me. 'No,' I said. He took my rosary collection, though, and a credit card, and pawed all over my papers in the bureau drawer looking for cash. He even looked at my will. Then he held me from behind—he was so *strong*—and walked me through the house. He asked about the presents I had wrapped for my grandson, but didn't take them. When his flashlight spotted my silver spoons in the wall rack he grabbed for them. Just before he left through the front door, he yanked the phone cord out of the wall."

I listened with my eyes on her face, but my vision was fixed on the action she described. I could hear his voice, see his face and body as it must have looked in the dark, illuminated intermittently by his flashlight. I could feel the weight of his body, smell his breath ("A sweet smell, like breath mints," she said). And I knew the terror of his groping hands and powerful grip.

The police who responded to Lucy's call did not treat her with the sensitivity I received from Mike Cristo. Instead of outrage at the crime and encouragement for her ("You're doing really well," Cristo had said repeatedly, acknowledging my shock and pain), she felt callously dismissed. She heard no words of support from the female officer, and the male officer who took her statement kept telling her she'd be "all right." They did not tell her to leave her house as it was, so they could get fingerprints (she cleaned her bedroom after they left), or follow up regarding where she would be the next day, as Cristo had done. How lucky I had been!

We talked on about how she has handled the aftermath of the assault. Friends and family encourage her to forget it, which is of course impossible. She absorbed all the encouragement I gave her regarding decisions she'd made for herself: a deadbolt on the basement stair door, a security system with a panic button, her insistence on staying where she was. I encouraged her to contact Rape Relief, to keep talking about what had happened and to give herself all the time she needed to heal. Like her husband's death after forty-three years of marriage, this was an experience she would never forget.

She asked about my assault, wanted to know the details. It was not difficult to tell her. I was conscious of wanting to minimize it for her sake, but she persisted in her questions and concluded afterward that my experience was much worse than hers. "Well," I offered, "suffering is suffering, and fear is fear. They can't be measured and compared, a cup of mine against half a cup of yours."

Finally we turned to our pieces of cake. The china plate and the spotless house made me think of my mother. Alone, would she have been as able to look the horror square in the face, and talk of it so plainly? And to a stranger? The answer surprised and comforted me: *Yes.*

Lucy and I compared observations about Slater, like two girls sharing a wicked secret. I told her much of what I knew from the detectives. And we talked of Peters and O'Brien as well, agreed that they had been always thorough and kind and unexpectedly considerate. Lucy told of her "puberty hair" collection in the prosecutor's office. "What color do you want?" she had called to Peters through the bathroom door. "Gray? Red? Black?" We laughed at the thought of his blushing face, of Whitman's giggle.

"But I don't understand why they let him plead guilty to just the burglary and dropped the indecent liberties charge," Lucy said of the prosecutors. "Why did they let him get away with that?"

"I don't know the answer," I said, trying to imagine the cautious give-and-take of plea bargaining. "But your case against him—just the burglary—will increase his sentence by several years. I'm grateful for that." My words were a feeble offering; how bruised and dismissed I would have felt had my rape been bargained away.

It was 3:30 and time to go. She hugged me good-bye. She is tall, and I must have seemed very small to her. Twice she asked if I would call on her again. "You can count on it," I answered. "I can't promise when, but you'll see me again."

13

FINAL BLOWS

After such knowledge, what forgiveness?

—T. S. Eliot

SUNDAY, NOVEMBER 6

The return to standard time has abruptly rearranged daylight and darkness to February levels. When I drove to the laundromat this week the wind and rain and sun were alternating as they had that Tuesday morning. I wore a sweatshirt and my button Levi's, and my burgundy parka.

Is it any surprise that I was jumpy, or that I looked at the two men who came and went while I was there as though I would have to identify them later? When for the third time that morning tears stood in my eyes, I knew I needed help. I tried to push away the need as I drove out of the parking lot, then turned left toward Margaret's office.

And she was there, instantly setting aside her accounting, as though nothing else were more important, as though she were expecting me. She showed me the letter she had written to Judge Kaye about the sentencing decision he must make, over

173

two pages long. Every simple, direct sentence plainly declared that she has been profoundly affected, that her life, like mine, will never be the same. Handing me that letter to read, she said without words: You do not suffer alone. Give the pain to me.

Last night I dreamed about Slater. The setting was a presentencing meeting, in a bare room around a large table. He sat at one end, closest to the door. His hands were interlaced in front of him; he was dressed as he had been at the trial, without the tie. To his right was his defense attorney, Joan Miller; to his left were the prosecutors, Vince Marcone and Pam Whitman. I sat to their left. There were two other men whose presence I dimly felt. Marcone, Whitman, and Miller were engaged in an animated discussion, full of gesture and inflection. The rest of us watched silently. Their energy overtook them and they all left the room, talking madly, making deals. The other two men evaporated. I looked down the table at Slater, feeling small, afraid, and confused. He looked over my head, then stood up and walked out the door. He was free.

Seattle, Washington
November 1988

Judge Howard Kaye
King County Courthouse
Seattle, WA 98104

RE: SENTENCING OF STEVEN ANTHONY SLATER

My name is Margaret Newberry. I have been a close friend of Migael Scherer and her husband, Paul, for eighteen years. We know each other's parents, brothers, and sisters. We are like family. For the past two years Jack Martin, another old friend of theirs, has been my sweetie. I mention that because Jack and I have played leading roles in the first line of support for Migael, and Paul as well.

On February 9, Migael was attacked by Steven Slater.

Jack was the first person she reached after she returned home from the police station. When they picked me up and told me about the attack, I didn't really comprehend all of what I heard. Then I saw the heart-shaped cut in Migael's neck. It was sickening.

Migael physically survived the attack (barely), but emotionally she has been stripped of a great deal. I know the sequence of events in detail. The charges of rape and robbery don't include the worst part of what Migael experienced. The thing that has so damaged her was being strangled to the point that she heard herself dying. She has an unshakable memory of hearing herself "gurgle" to death. She said at the trial that she was "leaving . . . going." Her escape from the attack would be to die. Then Paul came into her mind and she found strength to hang on a little longer. She relaxed to save her strength. For whatever reason, when she relaxed, Slater released his grip on her neck.

Slater is a thoroughly evil person. I have speculated how a person gets to be like him and I suspect there is a sad story if the truth could be known. Nonetheless, the man is out of control and extremely dangerous. He is fully capable of committing murder. He is a repeat offender, shows no remorse, doesn't acknowledge his actions, lies habitually, and seems to be an all-around scumbag. He is sick in a way that is rarely, if ever, cured. When he is back on the streets he will repeat the kinds of things he has done in the past. I fear for revenge on Migael. I fear for myself. I live close to Ballard and shop, bank, and often eat out there. Lots of my friends live there. One of my friends lives one block from Slater's aunt. Her neighbor knew Slater as a child and said he was always causing trouble even then.

I plead with you to put this man behind bars for the maximum sentence. I have heard that thirteen years is being considered. I wish a life sentence was an option. If you can increase the sentence higher than thirteen years, it would help so very much. He'll be back in Ballard some day, which frightens me enormously.

Sincerely,
Margaret Newberry

TUESDAY, NOVEMBER 8

I rarely show emotion in Judy Burns's office, but this morning my tears flowed easily; I worked to stifle my sobs.

"I don't understand this," I said. "I should feel triumphant, not empty." I pulled another tissue from the box on her desk, dropped the soggy one in my fist into the trash can.

"Forget 'should.' The trial was hard. It cost you a lot."

"I feel so weak, like I'm on the bottom of the food chain."

"Of course you do. You're exhausted. The outcome of the trial doesn't take that away, or the anger." I looked at Judy, my tears beginning to slow. "Up until the trial, you had a purpose, a goal. You said it yourself—you had to stop him. Now that's done; it's natural that you feel empty. And from what you're telling me, you're noticing some of your losses for the first time. Go ahead and mourn for as long as you need."

"Are you sure you don't have a recovery chart in your desk somewhere?" I asked, smiling a little.

"No chart, no plan," Judy answered. "Just time and work. Now, tell me how you've been taking care of yourself since the trial." Slowly, I explained. I described the soothing domestic routines, the comfort of friends, the hours of deep sleep. Slowly, she helped me recognize where I am strong, what is within my control and what is not.

When the hour was up she rose, but this time she did not reach for her keys. "Thank you for testifying," she said, opening her arms. "May I give you a hug?"

FRIDAY, NOVEMBER 11

We escaped to Brad and Helen's last night. The air in Port Townsend was cold, damp, and clear, full of the scent of evergreens and salt water. With Helen I felt as ever an immediate affinity. Here is someone as helplessly adrift as I am. Of course, the aftermath of her chemotherapy is still uncertain and threatening, despite the hopeful prognosis of her doctor. But it helps us feel less alone to note the similarities in our experiences. Both of us have survived procedures we could not control but which we willingly accepted. Both of us are disoriented in time, have been hurt by rejection and heartened by love, are confronting our own mortality. We ride different but parallel currents, and speak a clear, wordless language.

She and Brad also helped Paul resolve a dilemma regarding Gary and Sandra. Hoping to mend the friendship or at least understand why it has ended, Paul made a lunch date with Sandra yesterday. She broke the date and extended a dinner invitation for both of us tonight. Though Paul accepted, I knew as soon as I learned of the arrangement that I couldn't go. Their wordless withdrawal from me last June still hurts. Since that afternoon in their garden all their overtures have revolved around parties and public events. Not once during the thoroughly publicized trial did I hear from them. I try not to let their withdrawal harden my heart but cannot shake the feeling that Gary and Sandra want to see us only when we're up and happy. I am not ready to spend what happiness I have on them. Until I have extra to spare it is best for me to stay away.

For Paul the issue is complicated by his emotional strength; he wants and is able to express his disappointment to them. "It's not just Migael who needed their support," Paul explained. "I needed it too. I guess I just can't believe that they couldn't give it. I want to know why."

"Suppose you get together," Brad said, "and they're sorry

for what happened and want to resume the friendship. Would you want to?"

"That's a good question," Paul replied. "Right now, patching up that friendship would be a lot of work. I'm not sure I'm up to it. I know Migael isn't."

"Sounds like their friendship would be more of a burden than their indifference."

Paul nodded, still thinking. When we returned to Seattle he canceled the dinner date.

TUESDAY, NOVEMBER 15

Work on my sentencing letter to Judge Kaye has drained me. Listing all the ways I have been affected by the assault is discouraging, but it is also encouraging to know that—in this state at least—the feelings of victims and their friends are considered in the legal process. It is an incredible opportunity to tell the judge what I and so many others have suffered.

I reflect on the circumstances that placed us in that laundromat, Slater and me. He with his rage and his knife and his powerful arms, never saw the weapons of my words and my wits. Which of us, in the end, will be most devastated by that encounter?

Seattle, Washington
November 16, 1988

Judge Howard Kaye
King County Courthouse
Seattle, Washington 98104

RE: STATE V. STEVEN ANTHONY SLATER

On February 9 I was raped, robbed, and strangled by Steven Slater. I will never be able to forget how, in a brightly lighted Ballard laundromat, I walked into a trap while he patiently waited for my most vulnerable moment.

Blood, rape, and complete helplessness are terrifying memories, but for me these are secondary to Slater's nearly successful efforts to kill me. The stark fear I felt in those final seconds still grips me. This is brutality that defies understanding. There is no doubt in my mind that Slater's violence will escalate, some day, from rape to murder. It almost happened with me.

No single event in my life has affected me like those twenty minutes. The immediate effects reflected the assault itself: painful knife wounds, a crudely carved heart on my neck, bruises from his strangling thumbs and fingers, and a disorienting numbness. It was early March before I was able to be alone even for a few hours, and later before I could actually sleep. The flashbacks and nightmares continue, and many emotional wounds remain. Formerly outgoing and adventurous, I am now often withdrawn and remote. Slater has altered forever my faith in human nature and, I fear, my compassion for strangers. Even worse, he has dimmed my ability to reach out to help those I love. I miss so badly the enthusiasm and initiative I once took for granted. I will always miss myself as I was.

The months, even the day before the rape, I was looking for work as a teacher. All the momentum of my job search was derailed by Slater's attack. Not until mid-July was I able to work part-time as a technical writer, and even then the benefits were overshadowed by his arrest and the subsequent police and legal procedures. It will be a long time before I regain the resilience and optimism for teaching.

The outcome of the trial—Steven Slater's conviction —did relieve the dread I had been living with hourly since February. But my relief was soon eclipsed by subsequent news of paroled rapists who have become murderers. With the current recommended sentence of thirteen years Slater will be eligible for parole in perhaps eight. At forty-eight years of age he is likely to have kept his health, his strength, and his rage. Of course, people can learn from their mistakes. But I am afraid when I think what Steven Slater may have learned from this case: that the most damaging piece of evidence he left behind was not his fingerprint on a newspaper or blood on his jacket, but me—alive.

For all these reasons, most especially for all the women who should never be touched by the horror I have experienced, I ask you to consider the highest sentence you can.

Sincerely,
Migael Scherer

TUESDAY, NOVEMBER 22

Like all my morning encounters with Steven Slater—six of them this year—yesterday's went pretty much as planned. This one held the fewest surprises.

Margaret and I were the last to arrive in the courtroom. Lucy Gilbertson, in her cream-colored beret, smiled at me over her shoulder from the bench at the far end. I had expected to see her; Slater was to be sentenced for her burglary as well. She was surrounded on both sides by friends and seemed in good spirits. Those dear to me were seated near the doors: Chris and Paul, one row from the back, scooted over for Margaret and me; Maria from Victims Assistance and Kari from Rape Relief sat in front of us. It was the first time I noticed there were four rows.

Slater sat at a table next to his attorney, his back to us. In the six weeks since the trial he had grown a beard, a short, full beard that changed his chin line and covered his mouth but did nothing else to alter his appearance. His shoulders stretched the thin cloth of his red jail shirt. His hair had lightened somehow, had returned to the sandy brown and blond mix I had first seen so many mornings ago.

Of course, fear was waiting in that courtroom. It settled over me as I sat next to Paul, distorted all my perceptions. Pam Whitman smiled and walked toward me, asked me if I wanted to say anything to the judge. Though doubtful, I agreed immediately when she said it could make a difference. Behind my ears I could feel my pulse throb.

Judge Kaye entered and called the principal players to the bar. Slater walked toward the judge with that distinctive, springy saunter that makes no sound and that I shall always remember (like the springy walk of the man I had seen in the street last May, I thought suddenly). He leaned against the rail, shifting his weight to his left leg. The shape of his buttocks and thighs was clear through his dull red trousers. For a man about to be sentenced he seemed completely at ease. Joan Miller stood to his left, Whitman to his right.

Whitman opened in a clear voice I could hear easily. As she reviewed and outlined the case the door opened and Detective Peters walked in. His eyes panned the room, as though he were deciding where to sit. I felt a sigh escape, and my attention returned to the judge's bench. Then O'Brien entered, black binder in hand, same appraising gaze. He sat to Peters's right, in the front row. The fear did not subside, but my resolve steadied.

Both attorneys spoke about the length of the sentence. Whitman explained Slater's offender's score, which includes previous convictions for attempted rape and assault, and recommended thirteen years. Miller acknowledged my suffering but reminded the judge that the sentencing range took that into account, and recommended eleven years. Even with that, she pointed out, he would not see "the light of day" in his forties. I liked the ring of it, but not the recommendation.

Then the judge asked Slater if he had anything to say. "No," he said, in the completely unremarkable but familiar voice I had first heard when I was pinned beneath him on the floor.

Judge Kaye explained his right to speak, then asked again. "No," Slater replied, less audibly, and shook his head.

Then I was called. Though I could have spoken from where I sat, I didn't hesitate to walk forward. There was an instant's pause as I stared at the vacant space between Slater and Whitman and knew I could not occupy it. Whitman caught the fear in my eyes, shifted to the left and motioned me to her right. I rested both hands on the smooth oak rail, above waist height, and lifted my face to the judge. Though I was standing straight and rigid I knew I was the smallest person there.

"Good morning," Judge Kaye said. My face relaxed slightly. Then my plea: For all the reasons stated in my letter, I asked him to give the harshest possible sentence. He said he had read my letter, and asked if I had anything to add.

"No," I said. "I think I have said it all. I ask for myself and for Mrs. Gilbertson." He thanked me for my words and I returned to the back of the courtroom. Peters caught my eye and winked. I sat next to Margaret, trembling, and bowed my head.

Then, without fanfare or gavel, Judge Kaye delivered the sentence. His tone was almost conversational as he explained that he was rejecting the recommendations of both defense and prosecution. "This is a horrible crime," he said. "Here is this lady, minding her own business and bothering no one." He saw no reason for leniency, and set the sentence for count 1, first-degree rape, at 168 months. The highest in the range.

I exhaled audibly and leaned back into my seat. I could feel the smiles and relief around me, and barely heard the sentence for Lucy's burglary. Other conditions were added: All sentences to be served concurrently, no contact with victims, restitution (Slater owes me $52), credit for time served (four months to the day). Bail during appeal was raised to $200,000 ("The presumption of innocence no longer exists," Judge Kaye said pointedly). An appeal was filed, an expected routine Whitman had said didn't worry her; the case had been handled thoroughly by both sides, and should stand up well. Papers were shuffled and signed. The reporters who had been sitting in the jury box filed out. The *Times* reporter, whose coverage I had protested in my letter to the editor after the trial, glared in my direction. Everyone near me reacted immediately, eager to protect me.

The stir of all this distracted me for a moment from the unceremonious dismissal at the bench. When my eyes returned to Slater he had already turned around to offer his wrists behind his back to the guard. He was led out, without words or expression or a glance my way. Despite his red clothing he had become as quiet and unalarming as when I had first seen him. Perhaps it was the effect of his beard, just enough of a change for me to see him with fresh eyes. Or perhaps it was the procedure I had just witnessed; all the shark's jagged teeth had been pulled, and the new ones had not yet moved forward.

Numb and aimless, I was walked through the rest of the morning. All of us left in a bunch, past the reporters (Paul politely declined for me when one stepped forward) and into the elevator lobby. Maria did the arithmetic: fourteen years. He would be eligible for release in nine and a half, in 1997. And the sentence, at the high end, would count heavily next time. "Next time?" I asked. Maria smiled grimly and nodded. I looked to O'Brien and Peters, who merely shrugged. Chris offered the positive note when she said Slater would not be truly free until 2002. Ahh . . .

A tumble of remarks. Paul and Chris introduced themselves to Lucy. Maria reminded me about the Victim Notification program, suggested I sign up so that I would be informed when Slater is released or if he escapes, promised to send me the forms. Peters announced his plans to adopt Lucy as his grandmother. O'Brien offered predictions about Slater's future. An elevator descended with Lucy and her friends. "Give me a call, kid," she reminded me. For probably the last time I shook O'Brien's hand, and Peters's. Peters's left hand reached over to my shoulder, pressed briefly, barely. Everything had been communicated.

The little knot of us took the next elevator down. Kari got off on the fifth floor; more business as usual. Maria, too, moved on to another case. Chris and Paul continued on to work. I eagerly accepted Margaret's invitation to unwind at her house.

It didn't work. I couldn't retreat backward into Margaret's childhood, though I tried as I paged through the sixth-grade diary she had recently found in her mother's attic. As always after an encounter with Slater, I was caught in the helpless present. By the time Jack arrived for lunch I was crying in Margaret's arms. Jack embraced us both; neither said anything. The sky let loose and the rain fell loudly on the roof.

Jack called Paul for me. We waited and talked, and I seemed to steady. Just before Paul arrived another wave of tears arose. How little resistance I could offer against the surge.

As we drove home Paul did his best to distract me. He turned on the radio. He talked about how excited he was that I would be going to Hawaii with him next week, and how good the sun would feel after rainy Seattle. "Want to help me pick out some hardware for the aft cabin?" he asked, turning toward a lumber store.

I could only cry. Paul sighed, drew me close to him, shifted gears and headed for the marina. At home he held me until the sobs subsided and I could stand. He held me as we walked into downtown Ballard for a paper, and into Lombardi's for a glass of wine. Every time I needed him he was there with the right words or the right silence and his healing embrace.

Early, Paul made up our bed and we climbed in. Whenever the anguish rose he told me how brave I had been, and how smart. Yes, he admitted, I had been alone, and yes I would feel cut off from life for a while. But look at what I had helped others accomplish. And my efforts had yielded the best possible conviction and sentence—ones that would stick. Though all night I lay awake, replaying, shuffling and reshuffling the newer images with the old, wondering if I should have said or done anything differently, finally I was satisfied. Chris cinched it tonight when she passed on what Maria had said this evening when they met at the bus stop: It was the first time Maria had seen a judge exceed the prosecution's recommendation, and it was probably due to my letter.

TUESDAY, NOVEMBER 29

Finally, a full night's sleep. Only one slightly disturbing portion of a dream in which I attempt to load laundry. Unsuccessfully, as ever; the washing machines are too small, the dryers disgorge my damp clothes.

The previous three nights, three nightmares. In the first, a lean man with dark straight hair corners me against a chain-link fence. We are in a colorless, L-shaped yard. Equipment is strewn about. He presses a pipe wrench diagonally across my throat while I talk calmly of trivial things. He backs off, disappears. I follow through a maze of dead, living, and newborn rats.

The second morning, I wake to the sound of my strangled breath. I do not remember the dream that preceded it. And in the third, I watch through the eyes of a predator as he (?) prowls around and through a small house, watching its unwary occupants. Crouched under a crib, in the darkness of a bedroom, I hear a distinct whisper: "Mama?" Awake, my heart pounds wildly. I am damp with sweat.

All this no doubt the result of the fresh emotional assault of the sentencing one week ago, and the exhaustion of illness. Last Friday my doctor confirmed what I guessed and feared: The sound in my lower left lung that says what the X ray did not, the beginnings of pneumonia. Ironically, I am relieved to know that my lingering congestion and exhaustion have a physical cause. I think I needed confirmation that I really am run down and that I really do need to take extra care of myself. And that I desperately need a break.

It is a break I am taking now, and its effects are already noticeable. Paul and I have been in Honolulu since 1:00 P.M.

today. We have done little and planned less; his business meetings do not begin for several days. Since we arrived I have been relaxed, almost dazed, by the warmth and smiles and beauty around us. I am appreciating the freedom that allows us to do this. I am content to let events unfold as they will. I am content to let go.

14

SUBTLE SHIFTS

Words lead to deeds . . .
They prepare the soul, make it ready, and move it
to tenderness.

—SAINT THERESA

SUNDAY, DECEMBER 4

We made love early this evening, on the white sheets of the big bed. Our bodies glowed in the rays of the setting Hawaiian sun. The sky was all a soft lavender. Then for one long moment, in the midst of such beautiful intimacy, I became utterly separate. I began, almost, to leave my body.

It must have been the palm trees that triggered the sharp awareness of myself that I had last known beneath Steven Slater's body, my throat clenched by his tightening hands. Yet I was not now frightened, only startled. It was the image of a palm tree, and of Paul's face, that brought me back into myself and inspired the final effort that may have saved me ten months ago. This evening it was the reality of that same tree, and of Paul's embrace, that returned me to the world of love and safety.

THURSDAY, DECEMBER 15

All the rest and warmth of my week in Hawaii seem to have shaken off the illness that gained a foothold after the trial. Every day the congestion recedes. I barely notice it anymore. And somewhere during the last two months sleep has become delicious and restorative; only occasionally is it elusive or frightening.

Tuesday's mail brought Scott and Alice's "Super Citizen Award," and in last night's yoga class I did my first unassisted headstand and shoulderstand (ever, and at age forty-one!). For the first time since last February the gains are catching up with the losses.

Flashbacks of the *strangling* are now occurring around and during orgasm. As my breathing deepens and my heartbeat increases in Paul's tightening embrace, I hear the rasping, gasping sounds I made in Slater's grip. The arch of my body reaching for love and pleasure is, I know, the same arch my body made as it struggled in hopeless terror for life. And finally the letting go, the release into oblivion as my body softens and sighs. When Paul relaxes into me I think almost immediately: I *am* a very lucky woman.

WEDNESDAY, DECEMBER 21

Gloria wrote this week. Her words, so well intentioned, hurt deeply. Drop the obsession with the man who raped you, she wrote. It isn't right or healthy. Get the best professional help you can. We all want you back.

This is what she wrote, but the words between the words were louder. My sister does not understand, let alone feel, what I have experienced this year. To her it is something to "get over" as soon as possible, rather than to assimilate slowly and naturally. She is impatient with my pace. And, I fear, she is tired of hearing about *it*.

How could she have sent such a message? Were she to turn all those words back on herself she would stagger from the blow. I can understand that she has little room for my pain in her life; her son's illness is a heavy burden. But why this critical analysis?

So. An open line of communication has been blocked. I shall stay with "safe" topics when I write to her. I shall tell her what she wants to hear. I shall hide the wounds. Even from a distance she does not want to be reminded of them. I am deeply disappointed, and angry besides. Why is my family so afraid of my reality, almost every one of them? Only my mother has responded with gentleness and vulnerability. These are the qualities, I now realize, that she tried to pass on to us all, that my father's spirit has always overshadowed.

"Let them go for now," Judy Burns counsels. "Accept that this is who they are and who they are likely to be always. It's OK to keep the distance you need, as long as you need."

Still, I wish they had been there for me. Talking to my mother on the phone today, I warmed to her spirit and the sun that flooded the pilothouse. Is it my growing strength that makes it possible for me to feel this, or is it the strength in her?

SUNDAY, DECEMBER 25: CHRISTMAS DAY

The low winter sun blasts directly into my face as I sit, wrapped in the pink terry-cloth bathrobe Paul gave me for Christmas. We are alone this morning with our thoughts and the bright blue silence outside. I am astonished to have made it to this day. Although I'm still somewhat on the sidelines, I am conscious of participating in "normal" human activities for the first time this year.

It doesn't seem to matter that my participation is so limited. Decorating and gift exchanges have been minimal. I did not buy a single Christmas card, or bake breads, or make a present for anyone. Margaret's office party two weeks ago was the only party I attended; even there I became quickly exhausted by the light banter, and slowly worked myself into the corner of the couch where I was surrounded by cushions and the safest of friends. Nevertheless, the holiday season has affected me. It is as if, in setting aside all the outward flash and show, I have revealed the peaceful core. Unencumbered, that peace is settling over my spirit. Seeing how vulnerable I am, others temper their own frantic energy and approach me with gentleness. I am overwhelmed, not with glitter, food, and gifts, but with love.

We spent a couple hours with Jack and Margaret yesterday, sipping coffee and gobbling down cookies and talking about nothing of importance. On the floor Margaret wrapped a final present. As she tied the ribbon around the package I thought, this is the woman who walked away from her work last February 9, who comforted me the night after the lineup, who spent the week of the trial at my side. Seeing her wrap that gift for her sister, humming and giggling, she gave me once again the perfect present of her hopeful self.

THURSDAY, DECEMBER 29

I think my mornings of sleeping late, on weekdays at least, are coming to an end. This morning, despite the rain and the gray, I was vaguely impatient with myself as my thoughts jumped ahead to what I wanted to do today and even tomorrow. So this is what recovery can feel like: a quiet nagging to make a change anyone else would consider insignificant.

More ease than pain or wariness these days, but it is a subtle shift that can tip the other way unexpectedly. For the most part I am satisfied with my progress. I fix my sights on the tangible and near, and congratulate myself when I reach these carefully chosen milestones. Then the glimpse of a gray jacket, my own introspection, and I am removed, alone as I was when I looked out at the street from my prison of fear and violence in the laundromat. No hope of leaping from his powerful arms and through those barred windows then; my release waited on time and luck, on my wits and his inclination. I am not fully released, even now.

Is this sense of removal from life another lasting alteration, like my sharper awareness of possible danger, that I will slowly learn to welcome? In these moments I see myself as part of the stream, no more and no less important than anything else, and at the same time sense myself as utterly distinct. Because it recalls such horror, I am often overcome with sorrow. Yet what I am feeling as painful loss could as well be felt as an incredible gain. Is it so horrible, after all, to lose the false sense that I am important?

SUNDAY, JANUARY 1, 1989

A new year at long last. Felt great yesterday morning. I felt so *lucky*; lucky to have survived, lucky to have come through the legal ordeal with such satisfying results, lucky to be loved.

But as Jack, Margaret, Paul, and I settled in for a weekend stay on Whidbey Island, remoteness invaded my spirit. I wanted to look forward, but was trapped by the past. Why should 1989 be welcomed? I no longer trust the future. It threatens as much as it promises.

Halfway through the turkey roasting, the new year brightened. As I brushed drippings onto the bird, I thought, Why wait? I pulled the champagne from the refrigerator and found four relatively unchipped glasses in the cupboard. The four of us stood in a close circle and began our toasts.

We toasted everything: the new year, ourselves, dead parents and friends, the criminal justice system, good sex, cops, contortionists. We toasted, we sipped, we refilled our glasses. We grinned at our cleverness. We never sat down.

Margaret judged this the perfect time for the next ritual, which she called a "Navajo Circle." She and I culled the newspaper for upbeat headlines; we spread and taped those pages on the kitchen floor. I sat in the center. She drew a large chalk circle around me, with an opening for the evil to escape. Using different colors, she drew brown bolts of lightning near my arms (symbolizing thunder and strength), a yellow rising sun at my back, a pink heart in front of me (to keep my own heart soft), and many tears watering green trees. She strengthened my vulnerable left side with a rainbow of color. She grounded my feet with green and brown.

Neither of us knew what we were doing. But the more we talked and she colored, the more the circle filled out. The ritual was as silly as a slumber-party game and as serious as an exorcism. Not since childhood, when the pomp and mystery of the Catholic Mass enthralled me, had I felt the efficacy of ritual. As the one in the center of the circle, I was the focus of attention, receiving all its healing benefits.

This morning Jack and Paul built a bonfire on the beach. When it was good and hot I fed a pile of 1988 calendars into the flames. I flipped the largest calendar to the month of February and lay it on the very top. The pages blackened and curled, then ignited orange and red. I smiled, sighed, and felt triumphant. We poked the fire. I fantasized cruel and unusual punishments. I think we all did.

So the year was kick-started after all. Now, as Margaret put it, I can enjoy a break until the next significant date: February 9, 1989.

TUESDAY, JANUARY 17

Judy Burns is certainly right: This is a difficult period precisely because I am strengthening. Full of what I perceive as my old energy level, I attempt too much, weaken, and am carried backward by the current that is against me.

"Except for the sex," I said, though I hadn't intended to bring up the subject in my therapy session. Judy merely raised her eyebrows and nodded for me to go on. "It's still good, like I told you before. But lately, when Paul and I make love, I've been having flashbacks of the strangling as well as the rape."

"Is it ruined for you then?"

"No. That's what I don't understand. Those moments . . . when I was dying . . . come back, but at the same time I feel alive and safe and totally loved." I paused, trying to make it clearer. "I can see why it's called 'making love.' The rape . . . *that* was 'making hate.' "

"You know," Judy said. "Last summer, before the arrest, you said you needed to talk about what you felt when you were strangled. You described it as"—she looked up from her notes—"lonely."

"That's right. Sometimes it still feels like that. But not during sex. I wonder what that means?"

"Keep going with it. There's no reason you have to fight what you're remembering, especially if you feel safe. It's possible that what's happening with those flashbacks is helping you to heal."

FRIDAY, JANUARY 20

I finally answered Gloria's letter. "You can tell your sister anything you want," Judy had said when I asked for her advice. "But you can't control how she'll react." My reply—three pages of cheerful avoidance—was so cowardly. I may have driven the wedge between us a little deeper, but it was all I was capable of doing. This, then, is how we may begin to grow apart. Hurtful though well-intentioned advice offered on her part, withdrawal on mine. Where will either of us find the strength to mend the rift? And how will she know a rift has begun if I never tell her?

Unhappy with my letter, I turned to Paul, who was working blithely in the aft cabin. At least I had the sense to stop myself when I began to criticize his work. At least I had the sense to let the tears out when he embraced me. So many losses. So much to rebuild. And I knew exactly who to blame for it all, for the violence that tests and breaks. Slater's face took clear form, and I hated him with my whole heart.

I worked through the rest of the day to regain my balance. After dinner I forced myself to make a pot of coffee, hoping the heartiness would revive me and prevent me from crawling into bed at seven. Paul put a crossword puzzle in front of me at the table, and a pen in my hand. Mechanically, I began. Slowly, the mental distraction and the richness of the coffee took effect. As the puzzle filled out with my inked letters, my spirit lifted and steadied. And time in my cuddly pink bathrobe, and time making love and whispering in the darkness, and many hours of time in sleep—all, finally, restored me.

THURSDAY, JANUARY 26

Last night was broken by dreams and wakings. In one dream, I attempt to shave my legs with the blade of a scalpel. I am in high school, getting ready for a big dance. In a room full of showers, I cannot seem to find one that works. My legs are as hairy as a man's. I retreat into an old car with reclining seats. Through the closed windows many young men cajole and threaten. They want me to come out. I want to stay inside.

In another dream I sit at a desk, writing. The computer is so tiny my hands strike the wrong keys. The screen is almost impossible to read. I have so much to express, but cannot overcome the machine to do so. I work in a small, octagonal room, covered on the outside with cedar shakes. The entrance to this room is narrow and short, the width of my head and the height of my shoulder span. I am born into my writing room. Only men and women my size or smaller can follow me into it.

15

THE END OF
THE FIRST STEP

But, when the days of golden dreams had perished,
And even Despair was powerless to destroy;
Then did I learn how existence could be cherished,
Strengthened, and fed without the aid of joy . . .

—EMILY BRONTË

THURSDAY, FEBRUARY 2

It has arrived at last, this anniversary month, capturing everyone's attention with record cold temperatures. Yesterday the north wind blew snow through the cracks in the hatch; today the sun shone everywhere but melted nothing. Paul has been off work for a day and a half. Everyone is energized by the challenge of real winter weather. We are feeling snug and a little smug in our cozy home.

Climatic events have distracted me from my dread and anticipation of next Thursday, February 9. My mind returns to last year, to each day preceding that Tuesday morning. I recall my trip to Portland, breakfast with Anna in the Mallory Hotel. "Look at the color of this ring," she had said, showing off her azure stone. "This is the color you will see in the Caribbean." Our imminent trip, my own progress looking for work, all our plans for the new year—my outlook was bright in those days. Everyone around us appeared content, happy, hopeful. Friendships were coming together, life was easy and, thank god, we knew it.

Close by, within a mile of us, a man I had never seen before was about to turn forty. I cannot imagine him surrounded by hope and friends and smiles as I was. I cannot even imagine him smiling. Life must have seemed very dark to him. Unimaginable pressures must have been building: rage, hopelessness, distorted reality, pain. Soon, he would force all of these onto me.

SUNDAY, FEBRUARY 12

A year ago we were in St. Martin. We had just returned from watching the sunset and were eating the first of many delicious meals. I was dazed, feeling from a distance, amazed to be alive at all. Color and laughter dizzied me.

Today is cold and gray, yet even though my spirit is as flat as the light of this day, I am better, happier, stronger than I was one year ago in St. Martin. I can now say that to myself: One year ago life was far worse.

This year February 9 began with a nightmare. I had returned to bed after locking the hatch behind Paul, but instead of a few more refreshing winks of sleep I was gripped by a troubling, exhausting dream. I was in the parking lot at our marina, trying without success to fix the car. Filthy, I returned to the boat to shower. I could hear water running when I opened the hatch. My mother had just finished showering, so I quickly undressed and stepped in. Black grime streaked off my body as I soaped and rinsed, but all my satisfaction at getting clean turned to panic as I reached to turn off the water and it kept flowing from the shower nozzle. The shower pan filled and spilled onto the floor. The water pump cycled furiously. The boat would sink, or we would be out of water forever. Paul walked in and watched in disbelief as I stood naked, calf-high in water, crying that everything was out of control and ruined. I woke, gasping and afraid. The phone rang.

I had planned to accomplish something before meeting Paul downtown for lunch, but phone calls and my own buzzing thoughts distracted me. Paul called just before 10:00, and Chris just after 10:30 (from maintenance work at a police station, appropriately enough); the half hour in between crawled by as it used to for so many Tuesdays. I washed dishes. I let my mind wander. I noted with surprise that I felt great, if a bit anxious. The sun excited me.

My excitement increased as I rode the elevator up to Paul's office, then went to lunch with him and Chris. Chris's gift, a photo montage of all the "good guys" (O'Brien, Peters, Whitman, Maria, Kari), delighted me. I was the center of everyone's happy attention. Time had worked its magic, had brought us all one year past the horror. I had lived an entire year beyond the seconds I thought were my very last. It felt like a birthday. In a sense, it was.

Chris returned to work, but Paul and I headed for the public library. I needed to answer a simple question: What was on the front page of the newspaper *that* morning? What had Slater not been reading so intensely? When the film scanner reached Tuesday, February 9, 1988, the articles it displayed revealed nothing disturbing. Did he read his horoscope that morning? Was he encouraged in his "last-minute preparations for a career plan"?

For some minutes I stared at the magnified news page. It was as though I had uncovered an important key; Slater had chosen that paper as a prop, and it was a complete success for his purposes. A reader myself, I had been duped, lulled as I never would, perhaps, had he been simply sitting. But that same newspaper would later entrap him, would capture completely the unique whorls of his finger, placing him beyond a reasonable doubt in that laundromat that day.

I searched, in vain, for a subsequent news report of the assault. Well, it was one of many, no doubt, in a big city. So much for the eagle eye of the Seattle *Times* reporters. Where was their alarm for community safety then? I shrugged, expecting as much.

We moved to my next question: Is there a Ballard High School yearbook containing a picture of Steven Slater? I asked for the *Shingle* from 1964 to 1966.

Sitting at a bare library table with Paul at my left, I placed the 1964 yearbook in front of us. Its size and weight, the texture of its cover, even its smell, were completely familiar to us both. Our own 1964 books from our own high school were almost indistinguishable from this one.

To give me courage, to give it all a touch of the normal, I first turned to the Juniors section and looked for the picture of a friend I'd known in college. There was her smile that I have seen so often. There was her intelligent face. Her blond hair was banged and flipped, her eyes framed in white glasses. (I had discarded mine, almost identical, for contacts that year.)

"Here goes," I breathed, and flipped backward to the Sophomores. I nervously scanned the S's. His picture, no bigger than a postage stamp, filled the entire page.

His name was misspelled—"Steve Slatir"—but it was certainly he. The photographer caught him looking slightly to the right, the remains of a smile on his lips. The shape of his head, his ears, and his cheekbones have not changed, but the black-rimmed glasses and that slight, almost shy smile were features I would never see. His sixteen-year-old face held no clues of his encounter with me, or with his other victims.

Heart pounding loudly, I pushed the book toward Paul and opened the next, for 1965. Again I found my friend first. The caption under her senior picture listed Honor Society and French Club. Reassured, I opened to the S's among the Juniors of Ballard High.

In one year his face, like all the others on that page, like my own at that age—seventeen—had assumed its adult features. His hair, slightly longer now, was parted on the left. His mouth was set and closed exactly as I would see it years later in a bright laundromat, in the glare of a lineup, and in Judge Howard Kaye's courtroom. There was the short, slightly upturned nose and the indifferent gaze, heart stopping even behind his glasses. There was the man who would rape me, nearly kill me with his powerful hands.

I waited a few moments before opening the last book, caught my breath. Shock and fear had surfaced, but so had an incredible thrill.

The photographer had coaxed out that smile again. For his senior portrait "Steve Slater" was dressed like all the other young men who graduated that year, like all the other seniors in his yearbook, and in Paul's, and in mine: white shirt, bow tie, sports jacket. His list of activities—100 Mile Club, Ski Club, Boy's Club—spoke of afternoon runs through Golden Gardens Park, Saturdays to Snoqualmie Pass and Ski Acres on crowded smelly buses, car washes, and poster making.

So. Steven Slater did not spring up out of the ground that morning, just as he was not swallowed up whole afterward. Ballard, that section of Ballard most especially, was his past and his present. All the sidewalks, alleys, and yards, many of the neighbors and even some of the dogs, were utterly familiar to him. He as much as I belonged in that laundromat that morning. He had attended the high school nearby, had played in Gilman Park to the south, had roamed and explored all the area in between and beyond. Very likely he had prowled as well.

Our curiosity aroused, Paul and I paged through those three yearbooks. We pointed out the familiar and nostalgic to each other: bouffant hairstyles, pointed shoes, snug jeans and loose sweaters, short skirts and large purses. The girls wore eyeliner and pale lipstick; the boys wore their hair straight, short on the sides, longer on top. This was our high school era as well. Slater was a sophomore, Paul a senior and I a junior when the news of Kennedy's assassination spread through classrooms.

We all remember the Columbus Day storm, watched the Space Needle go up, learned to drive on the new I-5 freeway. We all remember the reality of the Vietnam War moving slowly into our lives.

All these parallels. Yet during those years Steven Slater was making different decisions, wandering different paths. Possibly his rage and his violence were already in place. The "Steve Slater" I saw in those yearbooks may have already taken the first steps that would place him twenty-two years later in a laundromat a few blocks away from where he sat for those photos. As the headline over his sophomore picture stated, those years truly represented THE END OF THE FIRST STEP.

I couldn't sleep that night. New mental snapshots to shuffle endlessly, new compost to shovel into the soil. But the peacefulness and safety I absorbed from the evening with Paul, Jack, and Margaret held back the panic. I was disturbed but not deeply afraid. In a sense, I had been reassured. It really is all random, unexplainable. Who could pick out the rapist or killer from those Ballard yearbooks? Who could predict his victims?

THURSDAY, FEBRUARY 23

I am squandering time every morning this week marveling at the space I awake in. We have moved into the fully remodeled aft cabin, are sleeping at last in our own stateroom.

Lying in bed with toes pointing astern, everything I see is finished and lovely. The overhead shines with new white paint. The oiled oak glows. The glass in the portholes twinkles. All is curved, smooth, and satisfying. Everything I see, every piece of wood, every hinge and fastening, was cut, fit and secured, shaped and filled, and finished by Paul and me. I am encased in a chambered shell of our own making, as beautiful within as without.

Yet my first night sleeping aft was not a good one. I dreamed of Anna's husband. His face, round, clean shaven, appeared to have been scrubbed and buffed. Death had done that.

"It's easy, being dead," he said to me from the opposite side of a large table. "It's not so bad."

"But what about the loneliness?" I asked. "Wasn't it lonely for you, the dying?"

He looked at me with eyes that said it was, and is. He looked at me with eyes that mirrored mine. He knew.

My sister, Gloria, will be here with us soon, down from Juneau for a college reunion. I am beginning to relax at the thought of her visit. I love my sister and don't want to hurt her, even by revealing that she hurt me, however unintentionally. Her life is hard, harder than mine. I am grateful for my growing strength, but I do not trust it. I plunge to the bottom unexpectedly. Fear, confusion, sadness, are just below the surface. How can I help her?

MONDAY, FEBRUARY 27

I just returned from the airport after a night and a day with Gloria. In our brief time together we somehow picked up the severed ends of our friendship and began to reconnect them.

It did not begin well. Last night, trying to explain why I felt the need to withdraw from my father (a need I barely understand), why I cannot yet bridge the space between us, I found myself pitted against her. "After his first response," I said, "I just couldn't be around him. It's still hard."

"But you know Dad," Gloria said. We sat on opposite sides of the main cabin. Paul was next to me. "He just can't talk about his real feelings. He doesn't know how to comfort. But he was hurt horribly by what happened to you. Now he's hurt by your reluctance to be around him."

"Why couldn't he comfort me?" I asked, my voice breaking. "I needed to hear the words! What has to happen to me before he'll say the words?" I struggled to be composed, as

Gloria was. "Anyway," I said, "I'm not responsible for his reaction to my attack."

"That's what Migael's therapist keeps telling her," Paul explained. "I think it's kind of a cop-out. Migael's not responsible for anyone's initial reaction, OK, but what about her reaction to that, and so on? It's got to end somewhere. We can't just write each other off."

"I didn't hurt him!" I cried, "I'm not to blame!" I felt like a child angrily protesting my innocence to adults who knew more than I. Paul put his arms around me, but I felt like he had moved to the other side of the cabin.

"I'm sorry," he murmured, holding me later in bed. "I didn't mean to hurt you. I forget sometimes that you're not strong enough to handle all this. I'm sorry."

So this morning I was wounded and shy, and afraid. Quietly, over our cups of coffee, Gloria made the first move.

"You never told me how you reacted to my letter," she said, without a hint of defensiveness.

"No," I said. "I was afraid to tell you." I exhaled slowly, decided to take the risk. "It hurt me. I wasn't ready for your advice."

"I thought about it a lot before I wrote," she said. "It's so hard, from Juneau, to know how you're doing. I hear things from others and it worries me."

"You've got to trust me," I replied. "Recovery is very slow. And it's not steady. I start to feel better, and then I slip all the way back again. But everyone assures me I'm doing well. It's scary, really, that this"—I pointed to myself—"is what doing well looks like. But it is."

She nodded, and we let the topic pass.

Needing exercise, we walked into downtown Ballard, ate breakfast, wandered through shops. Our talk wandered as aimlessly. The distances between us shifted and closed. By the time I drove her to the airport we were relaxed, laughing at the heavy traffic. I felt the warmth of her love when I hugged her good-bye. We could rebuild, in time. We had begun.

WEDNESDAY, MARCH 15

I am worried these days by the low feelings I am having about myself. It doesn't seem to matter if I do this or that, if I get out of bed at all. My point of view is so out of step that it is dismissible, even to myself. I am aimless. I have no compass; it is lost, and I cannot even bring myself to look for it.

Paul has noted an arrogance in my manner, and his pointing this out only deflates me further. I overreact to even the most minor attack and can understand how my defensiveness could be seen as arrogance. I no longer know how to act strong, let alone be strong. Paul's observations are painful, confusing, and right on target.

Saturday, as he worked on plumbing at the family home on Whidbey Island, I sank in a slow spiral of sadness and hopelessness. Most of that day I moved reluctantly, automatically. When I was not actually sobbing or fighting back tears I was dead inside. Who cares if I clean this area or not, if I cook this meal or make the bed? I can watch Paul solder and pound away, or I can stare out the window. I have no real contribution to make here. It all goes on, in any case, whether I am here or not.

I am beginning to understand the despair Linda expressed in our support group last summer, and the alarming statistic I stumbled across in the newspaper recently: Women who have been sexually assaulted or abused have a fifteen to twenty times greater chance of committing suicide. I wouldn't describe my own feelings as suicidal, but self-destruction is lurking in them. I feel small and worthless. Worst of all, I feel I'm in the way. My own ineffectiveness seems a stumbling block to others. I am reflecting on how everyone's lives would be today had those strangling hands persisted; I am concluding that they would be about the same. Sad and angry for a while, but then about the same. It is not that I am replaceable; it is simply that I am not necessary.

Friday night I dreamed I was being strangled, over and over. My sister, Gloria, watched passively. Somehow I was able to watch with her, as though I could move from my dying body to another, distanced one. When I could no longer move back and forth, when I realized I was trapped in the violence, I awoke. My eyes opened wide to the darkness.

MONDAY, MARCH 20

So this is depression. Judy Burns put a name to the sorrow and emptiness last Thursday. "Perfectly normal," she said, "and perfectly treatable." Where I was hurt and confused, she seemed energized, almost happy. Had she been waiting all these months just for this? Is it really so simple? For the first time she insisted on another appointment in a week, even walked me down to the receptionist to make it herself.

The dullness grew, woke me at 4:00 Friday morning. I got up angry with myself for not sleeping, angry about the inevitable weekend work at Whidbey Island. The dullness continued through breakfast with Chris and a visit to Jack at work. I didn't want to alarm them with the news that my spirit had taken a plunge. Mostly, I didn't want to alarm myself. By not speaking of it I could pretend it wasn't happening.

Stan arrived with Jason and Ben; Teri was staying home alone, taking a break from motherhood. We packed up the car and hitched on the trailer for the trip to the island. Wedged between the boys in the back seat, I listened to the drone of conversation, noted that I had very little to say. What did it matter, my opinion? Stan's resonant voice and Paul's chatter left no room for me. It would have required more energy than I could spare had I wanted to be heard.

All the week's careful planning, all the preparation that had cost me so much energy, all began to fall apart when we arrived at the ferry and learned that we were too late for the 5:30 crossing. Alarmed by the sight of the ferry pulling away from us, three-year-old Ben cried in Stan's arms.

"I know just how you feel," I told Ben. "It's scary when you feel left behind."

Ben saw my own tears and stopped crying abruptly.

When we finally arrived at Whidbey, I began to unload the car, distribute boxes and baggage throughout the house. I think I could have made it if it hadn't been for Stan's dog.

"What was in this?" Paul asked, holding up a casserole pan I'd brought from home. It was empty, licked clean of the meal I'd prepared the day before.

"Dinner," I said flatly, taking it and the box of food into the kitchen. "The dog must have eaten it in the car." Nothing matters, I thought. Why am I here at all?

I turned from Paul and walked into the bedroom. Without thinking I pulled off my clothes and crawled into bed. I cried into the pillow, then, when Paul joined me, into his shoulder, against his neck.

It is like an illness, like malaria; once it invades the body it never leaves. Grief and pain and terror are its fever. Slater's violence infected me, and all my healthy life fights against it. The struggle leaves me wasted, empty.

Paul brought me a cup of tea, turned on the electric blanket, tucked me in. The heat soothed and relaxed, and I fell into an exhausted, brief sleep. When he came to bed later I held him close, eased back into sleep again.

But the dullness woke with me, stayed with me through the morning. Like fog, it settled, lifted slightly, resettled. I cooked breakfast, watched Jason and Ben, attempted a small job or two. Dead inside, I wanted to disappear. As the clouds began to recede and the sun warmed the afternoon into blue and green, I offered to take Ben for a walk while his younger brother was napping. Exercise was what I needed, and distraction.

Ben put on his coat and bounced toward the road. I followed, shoulders sagging, feet heavy. A car sped by. "Stop!" I wanted to call out to Ben, suddenly afraid, aware that he was vulnerable too. How could I protect him? Halfway up the driveway I stood and could not move.

"Come on, Migael," Ben said. "Let's go." His three-year-old voice giggled. Seeing that I hadn't moved, he cocked his blond head, flashed his cutest, most teasing smile. "Come *on*," he repeated.

Still unable to move, I began to cry. His smile and eyebrows dropped into a frown.

"Are you crying, Aunt Migael?" he asked. I could only nod. He ran toward me, stopped some five feet away. "Who do you miss?"

The answer surfaced immediately: *Myself.* But I couldn't speak. I felt Paul's hands on my shoulders.

"Who do you miss?" Ben asked again, impatient, insistent, a little frightened. When I still did not answer he ran past me. I could hear him calling to Stan. "Daddy! Aunt Migael's crying. Make her stop!"

Paul turned me around and smoothed back my hair. He walked me slowly to the beach. Ben was already there, furiously throwing rocks into the water.

"Oh, honey," Paul said, holding me, rocking me. "Do you want me to stay with you?"

"I want to disappear," I said. "I feel so worthless."

"Don't disappear," he said. "I love you and need you around."

I nodded, accepting his words, struggling to believe them.

"Walk the beach with Ben," Paul suggested. "You can do it. Just put one foot in front of the other and walk. You'll feel better afterward. Ben!" he called. The little boy turned. "Take Migael for a walk. She's sad and needs to go for a walk."

Ben nodded solemnly as I moved toward him. I walked east a few steps, then west, then east again. "We're going this way," I said at last. We left the beach, headed up the bank.

The sun was on our backs as we walked the gravel road, casting shadows in front of us. Ben wandered ahead, trying to hide his shadow in mine. He took my hand when the trees closed in, released it when we walked in the sun again. His sing-song voice asked about birds, our destination, people in the cars we waved to.

"Why are you sad, Aunt Migael?" he asked. He was walking in the thick gravel on the side of the road, barely lifting his feet.

Both of us were pleased with the crunching results, as though it made our walking more important.

The answer was simple, but difficult to say.

"Someone hurt me," I replied, trying hard to control my voice. Above us a heron flew across the bay and into the trees, its legs trailing, its head thrust back.

"Did I hurt you?" he asked, still crunching the gravel.

"No, Ben," I said. "A bad man hurt me . . . a very bad man." For an instant I saw the face and form of Steven Slater, could almost feel him walking beside us. As quickly, he dissolved into the afternoon air.

Ben picked up a stick, threw it over the bank. "Let's *go*," he squealed, skipping ahead of me toward the dock. I followed, suddenly hopeful, inexplicably lighter. The fever had passed.

EPILOGUE

_____

JANUARY 1990

I never had a plan. It had never been, for me, a test I had to pass. My return to the laundromat where I had been raped and strangled was unexpected, even to myself.

It began when I saw my neighbor Ed leave his boat with a bag of laundry slung over his shoulder. The urge to follow, as strong as a homing instinct, surprised me. I was leaving soon myself, heading that way in fact. For the first time ever I knew it was possible and safe for me to go back. But should I? The urge subsided with the question. Suddenly indifferent, I decided to leave the decision to chance.

And it really happened that way. I wasn't trembling or anxious, just mildly curious when I glanced into the laundromat as I drove by. As always, the bright lights and large windows revealed everyone inside as clearly as a two-sided aquarium. Ed was standing in the far corner, hands in his pockets. Without thinking I circled the block and parked behind his blue pickup. Ignoring the barred windows I had looked through with such desperation almost two years ago, I walked to the side door and entered. I gripped the black pipe railing of the raised landing and looked directly at Ed, who was now leaning against the dryers across the room.

He blinked once—his only sign of surprise—and then he smiled, a small conspiratorial smile. "First time back?" he asked.

"Yeah," I said. "I saw you through the window as I was driving by. How do I look?"

"You look like you're in shock," he answered, and walked around the island of washing machines toward me as I descended the stairs into the laundromat.

How did I feel? From the instant I had entered my pulse raced and my stomach contracted. Even from the door everything was powerfully evocative: the angle of the light, the temperature, the sounds of the machines, the smell. Hyperalert, I noted and dismissed the two other people in the room, the strawberry blond reading against a washing machine and the slender, dark-haired young man who was busy at another. Disoriented, afraid, exhilarated, I was also a bit disconnected from my body. In shock.

"Shall we walk around?" Ed asked, offering his right arm. This touch of unexpected gallantry, so at odds with the feelings building within me, took me by surprise. I slipped my hand into the crook of his elbow and held on. His physical reality and playful formality steadying me, we walked—almost marched—past the dryers, past the utility doors, over the floor. My eyes darted everywhere but rested on nothing. My mind was moving so fast it felt blank. My body was remembering everything. There I had stood, slightly bent, loading those three dryers. There he had sat, legs crossed, patiently waiting. There we had struggled. There he had forced me to open the door. My left side knew the hard coolness of the linoleum floor, my right hand the smooth roundness of the doorknob.

Ed stopped at the vending machines and we stepped apart. "So where were you headed?" he asked.

Arrested by his question, I looked up into his face and stammered. "I'm on my way . . ." I began. Where was I? *When* was I? Ed's blue eyes anchored me into the present; all my anxious energy could not break their palpable hold. "I'm on my way to pick up tickets," I forced myself to say. My breathing was shallow. My heart was pounding. I must have looked crazed. I smiled at my feeble efforts.

"Tickets for what?" he asked. Though his face looked almost amused, his eyes continued to hold mine fiercely.

"For a play." I tried to think about my words, to arrange them logically. "A present. Paul's sister gave us tickets to a play. I'm on my way to pick them up, and saw you in here, and it just happened, it seemed the right time."

At once Ed's entire face softened, and he drew me into a quick hug that said everything I needed to hear about approval and understanding. Around us dryers roared and washing machines churned. Someone else—a woman, I think—entered, and with her the sound of wet traffic outside through the briefly opened door.

"I think it was a good idea," Ed said. "How are you feeling?"

"Incredible. The feelings are very powerful." My eyes filled with sudden tears I wiped away mechanically. "Could we step outside for a minute?"

We walked in the drizzle to the corner and back, then on around the block.

"Jesus," Ed said, mostly to himself. "It must be so hard." He meant everything, of course, but I was suddenly reminded that this was the first time he had seen my actual struggle. I had walked into his afternoon unannounced, grateful for his presence, somehow certain that his response would be the one I needed. My head clearer now in the gray cool air, I felt my attention shift to him.

"I've only had one experience even remotely like this," he continued, "when I was a new cop, moonlighting as a uniformed bouncer in a downtown bar." A fight had broken out, and he had botched it—ended up getting hit, losing his gun, the whole catastrophe. "I was so green," he said. "The worst part was going back to the same bar the next night, after losing control like that. No one was very happy about it, but the bar had to have someone like me in those days, and I was it. Jesus." Ed shook his head at the embarrassment—and more—it had meant. "But it's not the same."

No. And yes. I liked the story, liked the way it had taken me back to the time when Seattle bars served women only if they were seated in booths, before the World's Fair, when I was in high school. I liked imagining Ed back then, just starting out on a career he would retire from years before I met him, learning the hard way as we all do. Learning something important.

"Ready to go back in?" he asked at the front door of the laundromat.

"Yes," I said. "I'd like to go in, and out, and in once more."

Inside the atmosphere was still charged, radically different from any other spot on earth. The air was thicker, more difficult to breathe. I felt submerged and small. I watched silently as Ed emptied his laundry into a wheeled basket. I followed him to the dryers I had once used, focused on his quick moves as he loaded the damp clothes and inserted quarters in the coin slot. How effortless it was! I kept my mind on the present moment as my stiffened body remembered what had happened in this same small space: the hard, encircling arms, the sharp knife, the sticky blood, the low voice. I kept my eyes on Ed.

We moved to the side, windowed wall, and I looked around for a moment, breathing deeply and deliberately.

"So what does shock look like on my face?" I asked.

"Red in the middle, and white all around," Ed answered, gesturing around his own face. "You look better now. How's your pulse?"

"Slower. I feel calmer. But a lot is going on." I looked around again. "You know, this room is wider than I remember. It's as though it's been pushed into the street. And it's so bright and clean."

Ed pointed out the padlocks on the corner doors, and I remarked that the door leading to the room behind the dryers was narrower than the other, something I had never seen before. In my memory that door had become enormous. The tables seemed smaller, the benches almost insignificant. Somehow I had expected the laundromat to be transformed, altered forever by the violence, like a battlefield. But it was not. The smears of my blood had long been washed from the floor. The walls had swallowed my muffled gasps and desperate whispers. And had I peered through the windows into the narrow room behind the dryers, all would have been in place, the white metal chairs wiped clean and set upright, as though nothing important had ever happened there.

We left the drying clothes and walked to the corner deli. Silence punctuated our talk. Sipping coffee from Styrofoam cups, at a plastic table with a tin ashtray, we were together in a moment of complete communication. I felt alarmingly fragile, but nothing in Ed mirrored this feeling back to me. Instead, he looked at me with the mixture of calmness and unobtrusive strength I have seen before: in the police officer as he took my statement at the precinct, in Margaret as she watched me testify, in Paul as he rose to lead me from the courtroom.

My final return to the laundromat was brief, just long enough for Ed to stuff his dry laundry into his bag, just long enough for the helplessness to return. Overwhelmed, tears flooded my eyes as soon as we stepped back out into the drizzle.

"Are you going to be OK?" Ed asked, looking at me closely. "Yeah," he said to his own question, as though he had quickly assessed everything. "You're doing just fine." I smiled and nodded, and he hugged me with his free left arm. Beneath the laundry bag slung over his right shoulder his back was warm. We moved to our separate vehicles, and our separate afternoons.

Had it been worth it, going back? At first, everything I gained seemed like a loss. Going back forced me to let go of something I never knew I had been holding on to: the simple illusion of place. Unbelievably, that laundromat *is* a safe place, as busy and bright as any place anywhere. Nothing intrinsically dangerous about it. A very unlikely place for a rape, as the detectives had remarked. Only dangerous that morning, only dangerous because of one angry man with a simple plan. So I am reminded once again of the danger of any place, at any time of day. The neighborhood I walk through is a potential minefield. My home is a setup. No place is safe.

As time passes, gains emerge that feel like gains. The benefit of facing fear, for one. Ed spoke of this that day, but I was too distracted by the feelings of fear to understand. Now I think I do. In returning to the place where the terror once lived, I allowed the fear to surface. Not the real fear, of course. Just a reminder, like a souvenir. The important difference is that this time I was in control, however weakly. I chose to be there. I stared the terror down, not bravely, perhaps not wisely, but I was able to stare it down and move on. Afterward, my nights did not explode into nightmares nor my days into flashback, as they used to. Fear still lives within me, but I am heartened by this sign of recovery.

Going back showed me the reasons I am recovering. Some of these reasons have to do with me. Some of them have to do with others who, like Ed, have accepted my experience into their lives and patiently trust me to integrate it, at my own pace and in my own way, into my own life. Evil is real. Good is just as real. Going back, I gained the strength to keep going forward.

ABOUT THE AUTHOR

Migael Scherer is a technical writer and educational consul-
tant. She taught journalism and English in local public schools
for ten years and computer information systems at the university level in Alaska. She and her husband live on a boat in the
Seattle area.

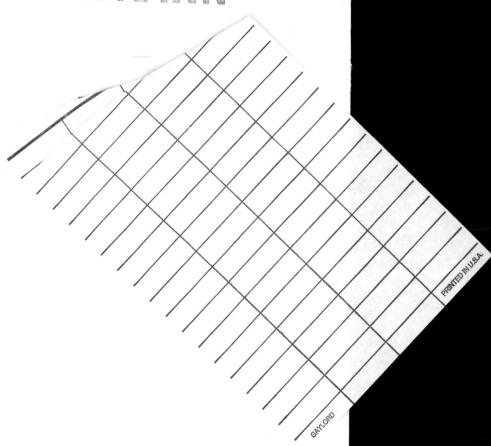